# FROM

# ASSOCIATE

# TO

# AMBASSADOR

The Distinctive Skills
Every Law Firm Associate
Must Master
to Enjoy an Exceptional Career

## Jeff Baldassari

*From Associate to Ambassador, The Distinctive Skills Every Law Firm Associate Must Master to Enjoy an Exceptional Career*

Copyright © 1993, 2023, Jeff Baldassari

ISBNs:
Paperback 979-8-9886619-1-7
eBook 979-8-9886619-0-0
Audiobook 979-8-9886619-3-1

Cover Design by Edge of Water Designs, edgeofwwater.com
Typesetting and eBook Design by Iryna Spica, irynaspicabookdesigner.ca

# Prelude

It's been 30 years since I wrote the manuscript for this book. Despite the seismic changes that have occurred in the world and in the practice of law, the content has stood the test of time. When my career shifted focus and I stepped into the role of mentor, I realized that there was no similar resource that effectively communicated these crucial skills for the practice of law. I knew the time for this book had come.

Foundational values and principles are timeless. They endure for generations and their impact resonates just as strongly today as it did in 1993. Therefore, rest confident that the contents herein are not simply the "next big thing" in legal practice. They are enduring truths that will benefit you immediately and serve you well throughout your entire career just as they have served those who have come before you.

I never intended this publication to be a how-to book. It doesn't contain any rules of substantive law. It is simply a collection of best practices drawn from observations, and it will provide you with an interactive experience to embed these practices into your career journey.

The approach is simple. If you incorporate these principles into your professional habits, the impact on your career will be profound. I have stripped away any narrative that could easily have been included so that the subtleties of the observations are not buried in the text, consequently increasing their impact.

I didn't conceive all of these concepts on my own. I, like all of us in this profession, applied what I observed or learned from my mentors. Therefore, I must give special recognition to several talented attorneys who impacted my professional development tremendously far beyond the practice of law. I was fortunate to work with these professionals when I practiced law and I benefited from the experience. Thank you Richard R. Hollington Jr., Lawrence V. Lindberg, Thomas R. Lucchesi, and J. Kearney Shanahan.

Jeff Baldassari
November 2023

# Introduction

Accelerating the trajectory of a career is not a passive endeavor. It requires a strong sense of self-awareness followed by consistent action. This is not a perfect science with a guaranteed outcome. Rather, think of it as a journey: specifically, a journey without a destination. Continuous learning and improvement require you to have an insatiable appetite for improvement and to accept the fact that you will never "arrive." When one goal is achieved, a higher one must be set. Contentment with the status quo is death.

I suspect that you purchased this book not because you want an ordinary career in the practice of law. I think that you aspire to achieve more. How that's defined is personal to you. I surmise that you want to be more than just a partner in a law firm with expertise in a field. Perhaps the role of ambassador to the firm is more to your liking. You want to bring something much bigger than yourself to the table. That's where professional fulfillment lies, and it's yours for the taking.

The key to your success is people, specifically, your connection to them. Your ability to influence, inspire, motivate and manage people is everything. People buy from people. People support people. The common denominator in successfully achieving these outcomes is trust and respect.

Trust and respect are earned. Both require time and consistent effort from you. This book will help you in those efforts. I provide you with specific, actionable tasks or points to consider to both get you started and keep you going. Each task is accompanied by a recommended activity to develop your skills and inspire you to greatness. Along the way, I encourage you to monitor your progress and check off your accomplishments. Through these core concepts and takeaways, you will enhance the level of your practice and improve the quality of your relationships with clients, peers and support staff.

Enjoy the journey!

# Table of Contents

*Everything in life is easy until people get involved.*
FRED J. BALDASSARI

# GENERAL SKILLS

Certain skills permeate all professions and industries. Such skills form the cornerstone on which technical skills are founded and developed. Not only do these skills enhance the value of the individual attorney, both personally and professionally, but they also have a synergistic effect on coworkers. To be sure, the overall impact of mastering these general skills is dispositive to the successful practice of law.

## GENERAL SKILLS

- Motivation That Moves You
- Be Responsible for Your Own Success
- No Man Is an Island
- Self-Management and Personal Growth
- A Skilled Writer Is a Skilled Communicator
- A Matter of Ethics

# Motivation That Moves You

Although necessary in nearly every profession and industry, motivation and personal disposition are especially crucial in the practice of law because you are an extension of your client, serving in a leading role. You, not your client, are the driving force. As a result, a proactive approach driven from within is a must.

Not only do the following skills enhance the performance and value of the individual attorney, both personally and professionally, but they also have a synergistic effect on coworkers.

By leveraging your personality to your advantage, you will bring out the best in yourself and your team to achieve extraordinary results consistently.

# Possess an Excellent Attitude

*A positive approach is always better than a negative one.*
HERBERT E. MARKLEY

Throughout your entire career, you will need to overcome challenges and obstacles. Your attitude sets the stage for what's possible and for envisioning a successful outcome. It's imperative from the start of the engagement that you believe the ultimate goal can be achieved.

*There is no medicine like hope, no incentive so great,*
*and no tonic so powerful as expectation of something better tomorrow.*
ORISON SWETT MARDEN

Ask yourself: How have I achieved positive outcomes in my life and career when I faced less-than-ideal circumstances?

_____

_____

_____

_____

What made me believe that I would be successful?

_____

_____

_____

_____

*An optimist is a man who says the bottle is half full*
*when it's half empty.*
AUTHOR UNIDENTIFIED, *NEW YORK LAW JOURNAL*, JUNE 11, 1962

# Perform Your Work with Enthusiasm

*Enthusiasm is the natural expression of*
*finding the good everywhere and trying to bring it to others.*
JOSEPH B. TRAINER

Enthusiasm is contagious. There's nothing more empowering than the belief that an outcome can be achieved. When a team fully embraces the possible, magic happens.

*If you aren't fired with enthusiasm,*
*you will be fired with enthusiasm.*
VINCE LOMBARDI

How do you "fire up" your teammates?

_____

_____

_____

_____

List a few different approaches.

_____

_____

_____

_____

_____

*A man can succeed at almost anything*
*for which he has unlimited enthusiasm.*
CHARLES SCHWAB

# Become Physically and Nutritionally Fit

*A man too busy to take care of his health is*
*like a mechanic too busy to take care of his tools.*
SPANISH PROVERB

To be at your professional best, you need to be healthy, both physically and mentally. If you neglect your body and mind, your performance will be subpar.

*Most of us are not going to wear out—we'll rust out from inactivity.*
*Optimum nutrition, sufficient sleep, regular exercise,*
*moderate drinking, no smoking, limited stress, correct weight—*
*put them all together and they spell superior health.*
*Carefully followed, this kind of program can perhaps expand our life span*
*toward the 100 to 120 year range some scientists consider possible.*
*Suppose that happens. What could we look forward to?*
*Titian did superb work until near his death at age 99.*
*Pablo Picasso was turning out masterpieces well into his 90s.*
*Roscoe Pound wrote a five volume work on U.S. jurisprudence*
*after his 95th birthday.*
PAUL MARTIN

What is your physical fitness regimen? How well do you stick to it?

How conscientious are you of the foods you consume and beverages you drink?

*I believe that the greatest gift you can give your family and*
*the world is a healthy you.*
JOYCE MEYER

# Possess, Exhibit and Utilize Uncommon Energy

*Human vitality is so exuberant that in the sorriest desert it still*
*finds a pretext for slowing and trembling.*
JOSÉ ORTEGA Y GASSET

It's your responsibility to bring the energy. Don't expect it to happen on its own. You are the catalyst that "lights the fire" and keeps it lit.

*Energy and persistence conquer all things.*
BENJAMIN FRANKLIN

How do you ignite your inner energy and keep it flowing? Who do you know that possesses uncommon energy? Which of their actions/traits/activities can you mimic?

_____

_____

_____

_____

_____

_____

_____

_____

*Energy is beauty—a Ferrari with an empty tank doesn't run.*
ELSA PERETTI

# Be Driven

*What would life be if we had no courage to attempt anything?*
VINCENT VAN GOGH

The force needed to overcome challenges comes from within. You will be knocked down and pushed around multiple times in your career. It's your inner drive that empowers you to get up and find a way to persevere.

*If you let conditions stop you from working, they will always stop you.*
JAMES T. FARRELL

Who do you admire for their ability to push forward? How are they able to overcome setbacks or achieve "the impossible"?

_____

_____

_____

_____

_____

_____

_____

_____

_____

_____

*Persistency is the jewel.*
ALPHEUS THOMAS MASON

# Have Fun at Work

Fun is at the intersection of everything good in life, professionally and personally. It's an accelerant that brings out the best in you on multiple levels.

What makes your job fun?

_____

_____

_____

_____

_____

_____

_____

_____

_____

## MOTIVATION THAT MOVES YOU

- Possess an Excellent Attitude
- Perform Your Work with Enthusiasm
- Become Physically and Nutritionally Fit
- Possess, Exhibit and Utilize Uncommon Energy
- Be Driven
- Have Fun at Work

# Be Responsible
# for Your Own Success

You're in charge of your own destiny. Mentors can, and will, guide you, but in the end you're the one who decides the road to travel and must accept the consequences. Don't leave it up to others. To others, giving guidance is an academic exercise in which they can cast an opinion without experiencing much consequence. It's up to you to make informed, intentional decisions regarding your career. Own it.

# Strive to Become
# a Well-Rounded Individual

*Few people do business well who do nothing else.*
PHILIP DORMER STANHOPE

Having hobbies and activities outside the practice of law expands the world around you. It helps you see things from different perspectives and makes you a more interesting individual.

*A lawyer without history or literature is a mechanic,*
*a mere working mason;*
*if he possesses some knowledge of these,*
*he may venture to call himself an architect.*
WALTER SCOTT

List your hobbies and interests outside the practice of law:

_____

_____

_____

_____

_____

_____

_____

*If people are attracted to me, I like to think it's because*
*I'm an interesting person, fairly smart, well-rounded,*
*with a good sense of humor.*
*I would like to think that's what I am.*
*I would like to think people see it.*
ROB LOWE

# Appear Professional to Be Treated Like a Professional

*Personal appearance is looking the best you can for the money.*
VIRGINIA CARY HUDSON

Never underestimate the power of image. First impressions do matter, especially in a professional services industry. You must always "look the part." If you don't, you'll end up wasting time and energy trying to reverse inaccurate beliefs regarding your capabilities.

*People don't buy from clowns.*
DAVID OGILVY

Checklist to project your best image:

Have you purchased the best business wardrobe you can afford?

———

Do you keep your shoes shined and your wardrobe clean and pressed?

———

Do you look as sharp at 5:00 p.m. as you did when you arrived in the morning?

———

Is your office neat and organized?

———

*It is easy to be beautiful; it is difficult to appear so.*
FRANK O'HARA

13

# Annually Set Personal
# Short-Term and Long-Term Goals

*Without some goal and some efforts to reach it, no man can live.*
FYODOR DOSTOEVSKY

Every career needs direction. You must direct your efforts towards a desired outcome. It's a continuous multistep process, but it's as simple as the question you were asked many a time as a child: "What do you want to be when you grow up?" If you can answer that question, then it's imperative you identify the steps required to achieve your dream.

*If you do not know where you are going, every road will get you nowhere.*
HENRY KISSINGER

Where do you see yourself in one year? Five years? Ten years?

How would you like to see your responsibilities grow?

What types of clients would you like to serve?

How do you want to be viewed by your peers? By your clients?

*My philosophy of life is that if we make up our mind*
*what we are going to make of our lives,*
*then work hard toward that goal, we never lose—*
*somehow we win out.*
RONALD REAGAN

# Make Things Happen

*Don't wait for your ship to come in: swim out to it.*
ANONYMOUS

A passive approach is a helpless one that leaves things to chance. Take control of your destiny by actively pursuing outcomes. By asserting yourself and leading others, you will achieve, accelerate and exponentially increase your success in life.

*The successful people are the ones who can think up stuff*
*for the rest of the world to keep busy at.*
DON MARQUIS

How often do you find yourself waiting for something to come to you?

_____

_____

_____

_____

Identify three things that you could do right now that would advance your position with a matter or in your career.

_____

_____

_____

_____

_____

*A wise man will make more opportunities than he finds.*
FRANCIS BACON

# Understand That Extraordinary Results Require Extraordinary Effort

*The reason a lot of people do not recognize opportunity is because it usually goes around wearing overalls looking like hard work.*
THOMAS A. EDISON

You must accept the fact that sacrifice will be required. There is always a massive gap between the present reality and your goals. You must build the bridge between the two. Your strength will be put to the test and you will have to find ways to dig deep to achieve the lofty goals that you set for yourself.

*Lawyers can earn a living by the sweat of their browbeating.*
JAMES GIBBONS HUNEKER

Think of a time when you really pushed yourself. How did you find the way to dig deep?

_____

_____

Where can you assert yourself more today?

_____

_____

*I was a freak. But I believe all major athletes must be freaks.*
*You don't get abnormal results from normal people.*
*The difference between modern track athletes and*
*those of the past is that now we have to be mental freaks as well.*
*A race like the four-minute mile requires an extraordinary*
*mental approach, a conditioning of the will.*
ROGER BANNISTER

# Take and Accept Responsibility

*I don't mean to sound arrogant, but it's my ass that's on the line.*
ROBERT S. HILLMAN

Taking responsibility is what great leaders do. People admire and trust those who take responsibility for the good and the bad. Deflecting responsibility is a sign of untrustworthiness.

*The price of greatness is responsibility.*
WINSTON CHURCHILL

When was the last time you took responsibility for a bad outcome?

_____

_____

_____

How did people react?

_____

_____

_____

What did you learn from the experience?

_____

_____

_____

*Responsibility, n. A detachable burden easily shifted to*
*the shoulders of God, Fate, Fortune, Luck or one's neighbor.*
*In the days of astrology, it was customary to unload it on a star.*
AMBROSE BIERCE

# Know Your Limitations

*Each of us has a day, more or less sad, more or less distant,*
*when he has to accept, finally, the fact that he is a man.*
JEAN ANOUILH

The only way you will know what you are capable of achieving is if you push yourself to the limit. Growth does not reside in comfort. Get outside of your comfort zone and you may discover that you are more capable than you originally thought. Once you reach that point, you will have a much better understanding of your strengths and weaknesses.

*You will never know your limits unless you push yourself to them.*
ANONYMOUS

When was the last time you pushed yourself outside your comfort zone?

_____

_____

What did you discover?

_____

_____

How often do you push yourself outside your comfort zone?

_____

_____

*"Know thyself" is an old saying: but who has ever known himself?*
WILLIAM LYON PHELPS

# Keep Mistakes to a Minimum and Don't Make the Same One Twice

*Failure is success if you learn from it.*
MALCOLM FORBES

Everyone makes mistakes. You will likely learn more from the mistakes you make or witness than from your successes.

*The greatest mistake you can make in life is to be continually fearing you will make one.*
ELBERT G. HUBBARD

What did you learn from the last mistake you made?

_____

_____

_____

_____

_____

_____

_____

_____

*We must be able, at any time, to accept the fact that we could all be absolutely and utterly wrong.*
TERRY PRATCHETT

## BE RESPONSIBLE FOR YOUR OWN SUCCESS

- Strive to Become a Well-Rounded Individual
- Appear Professional to Be Treated Like a Professional
- Annually Set Personal Short-Term and Long-Term Goals
- Make Things Happen
- Understand That Extraordinary Results Require Extraordinary Effort
- Take and Accept Responsibility
- Know Your Limitations
- Keep Mistakes to a Minimum and Don't Make the Same One Twice

# No Man Is an Island

The practice of law is a team sport, not an individual one. The team that you build around you will determine the magnitude of your successes and the trajectory of your career. The only way to bring out the best in your team is to create an environment in which they can excel. It's more about them than it is about you.

# Treat All Coworkers with Respect, Regardless of Their Position in the Firm

*Evaluate every idea on its merits, regardless of its source.*
C. PETER MAGRATH

The best way to influence people to work together to achieve a desired outcome is to treat them with respect. People who are respected become inspired and will often do more than what's expected.

*The single wisest thing I ever heard Roscoe Pound say was that*
*"people want to be who's not what's."*
HARLEN B. PHILLIPS

How do you see the value in the contribution of each of your teammates?

_____

_____

Do you find yourself starstruck with respect to people's titles?

_____

_____

Conversely, do you find yourself getting caught up in the education level of your coworkers? In other words, drawing conclusions on the basis of a degree or lack thereof?

_____

_____

*The best index to a person's character is*
*(a) how he treats people who can't do him any good, and*
*(b) how he treats people who can't fight back.*
ABIGAIL VAN BUREN

# Remember People's Names

People make all the difference in the world. Giving recognition to your coworkers daily says more about you than them. Your daily interactions have the power to draw others towards or push them away.

Do you recognize and interact with your coworkers each day?

_____

_____

How do you express your sincerity?

_____

_____

How could you expand your circle?

_____

_____

_____

_____

# Say "Thank You" Often

Gratitude is one of the most important emotions you can express. It makes others feel appreciated and it will maintain your mental health. We all know that money doesn't buy happiness. Gratitude does.

Do you maintain a daily gratitude journal?

_____

_____

_____

_____

How often do you express your gratitude to others?

_____

_____

_____

_____

# Be Punctual, or Call Ahead to Inform the Other Party

*Every art must be worked at and practiced.*
*I contend that the art of being on time is no exception.*
THE ART OF BEING ON TIME
PART 2, EDITORIAL IN FOLIO, JUNE 1977

Next to expressly insulting a coworker, nothing says "I don't appreciate and respect your time" better than tardiness. Wasting others' time reflects an unhealthy degree of selfishness. You are not the absolute that others orbit around.

*People count up the faults of those who keep them waiting.*
FRENCH PROVERB

How often are you late for meetings or calls?

_____

_____

_____

_____

What measures can you take to ensure that you are consistently prompt?

_____

_____

_____

_____

*The trouble with being punctual is that nobody's there to appreciate it.*
FRANKLIN P. JONES

# Be a Leader and a Team Player

*Managers are people who do things right,*
*and leaders are people who do the right thing.*
WARREN G. BENNIS AND BERT NANUS

Inserting yourself into the role of a servant leader is the best way to bring a team together. You may have the authority and responsibility to make the final decisions, but to achieve the best outcomes you must serve your team first. Empower them and create a safe environment for them to operate.

*Leadership is an action, not a word.*
RICHARD P. COOLEY

What actions do you take to support your team?

_____

_____

How do you demonstrate to your team that they are a priority?

_____

_____

How do you ensure that every teammate has what he or she needs to be successful?

_____

_____

*A leader who doesn't bend with every breeze may not be universally loved,*
*but he is very likely to be respected.*
MINIMAL RESPONSE,
EDITORIAL, WALL STREET JOURNAL, APRIL 8, 1980

# Take Time to Give Proper Recognition to Coworkers

*I praise loudly. I blame softly.*
CATHERINE II (CATHERINE THE GREAT)

The most powerful tool you can employ to inspire teammates is recognition. Consistently appreciating the contributions and efforts of others goes a long way. It's imperative that you communicate recognition in a sincere manner and in the setting that the recipient prefers. Conversely, your silence or only occasional comments will cause coworkers to feel undervalued. Praise should be given on at least a weekly basis.

*We all can't be heroes because somebody has to sit*
*on the curb and clap as they go by.*
WILL ROGERS

Take the time to find out how your teammates want to be recognized, publicly or privately?

_____

_____

Do you recognize coworkers for the little things that many people take for granted?

_____

_____

*I have always said that*
*if I were rich man I would employ*
*a professional praiser.*
SIR OSBERT SITWELL

27

# Learn from Others' Mistakes and Accomplishments

*To know the road ahead, ask those coming back.*
CHINESE PROVERB

Never forget that history repeats itself and there's no need to reinvent the wheel if you don't have to. You can learn the easy way by paying attention to others' successes and mishaps, or you can do it the hard way by thinking you're better or smarter than others who came before you.

*Wise men learn by other men's mistakes, fools by their own.*
ANONYMOUS

List the attorneys that you respect the most.

_____

_____

What lessons did you learn from them?

_____

_____

Keep a log of "things I should never do." Gather this information from situations in which others ended up with egg on their face.

_____

_____

*All of us must become better informed.*
*It is necessary for us to learn from others' mistakes.*
*You will not live long enough to make them all yourself.*
HYMAN G. RICKOVER

# Don't Burn Bridges

*And do as adversaries do in law—strive mightily,*
*but eat and drink as friends.*
WILLIAM SHAKESPEARE

In life, when you meet someone for the first time, you never know when your paths will cross again or whether this person will be someone who can help you in a future time of need. Treat each individual with respect. The last thing you need is an enemy. There are enough haters in this world. You don't need to intentionally add names to the list.

*The secret of successful managing is to keep the five guys*
*who hate you away from the five guys*
*who haven't made up their minds.*
CASEY STENGEL

How self-aware are you in your interactions with others?

_____

How fragile is your ego? Do you find yourself needing to get the last word?

_____

Are you capable of letting things go and walking away from a debate?

_____

*Be awfully nice to them going up,*
*because you're gonna meet them all coming down.*
JIMMY DURANTE

## NO MAN IS AN ISLAND

- Treat All Coworkers with Respect, Regardless of Their Position in the Firm
- Remember People's Names
- Say "Thank You" Often
- Be Punctual, or Call Ahead to Inform the Other Party
- Be a Leader and a Team Player
- Take Time to Give Proper Recognition to Coworkers
- Learn from Others' Mistakes and Accomplishments
- Don't Burn Bridges

# Self-Management and
# Personal Growth

When you graduated from law school, you attended a commencement ceremony. Taken literally, this event recognized the beginning of your intellectual advancement, not the end of your schooling. You certainly don't want to peak intellectually and professionally around the age of 25. It's up to you to keep advancing professionally and to embrace the concept of continuous learning and self-improvement. The opportunities to do so are numerous and readily available. Take advantage of them. Your career depends on it.

# Master Stress Management

*Preparation is one thing; panic is another.*
GUY FERGUSON

The practice of law is a pressure cooker. The source of pressure may be the timeline, the lives impacted, the dollars involved, the opportunities to be lost or gained or a combination of all. Pressure is a distraction. The best attorneys don't allow it to affect their performance because they maintain their focus on the tasks at hand and the desired outcomes, not the pressure. Pressure is an "action sport." You can't get better operating under it by studying it in a book. Keep putting yourself "in the game" so your comfort level rises under pressurized conditions.

*Winning comes down to who can execute under pressure.*
BILLIE JEAN KING

How well do you perform under pressure?

_____

_____

_____

Does it bring out the best in your performance?

_____

_____

_____

*Don't cross this field unless you can do it in 9.9 seconds.*
*The bull can do it in 10.*
SIGN IN A MIDWESTERN PASTURE

# Adapt Easily to Changing Circumstances

*We cannot direct the wind, but we can adjust the sails.*
DOLLY PARTON

We don't live in a static world. Everything is fluid and in a constant state of change. What worked yesterday may not work today because circumstances have changed. Most people are resistant to change, but the quickest and easiest way to excel is to embrace change. It's the law of life.

*Intelligence is the ability to adapt to change.*
STEPHEN HAWKING

Identify areas and practices that you have changed in the past few years.

_____

_____

Where are you stuck in your ways?

_____

_____

What changes have you witnessed in others that led to better outcomes?

_____

_____

*Enjoying success requires the ability to adapt.*
*Only by being open to change will you have the true opportunity*
*to get the most from your talent.*
NOLAN RYAN

# Maximize Use of Available Time

*The secret of a successful lawyer is that he makes use of all of his spare time.*
A. S. CUTLER

Who among us has not left a meeting and said, "There's an hour of my life that I'll never get back"? Administration matters can also be time sucks and mental distractions. The key to staying in the mental flow is finding ways to block out time to work on a project with no interruptions. Stopping and starting a task is inefficient, and it will be reflected in your work product.

*I know of no effective executive who has not made
a conscious point of managing his time as deliberately
as an investment manager his securities.*
LOUIS B. LUNDBORG

Reflect and identify where you lose time daily.

What changes can you make to eliminate that lost time and prevent interruptions from happening?

_____

_____

_____

_____

_____

_____

*A man that is young in years may be old in hours, if he has lost no time.*
FRANCIS BACON

# Distinguish the Forest for the Trees

*If you just focus on the smallest details,*
*you never get the big picture right.*
LEROY HOOD

At the start of every matter, visualize a vivid picture of the desired outcome. From that point, plan backwards to the where you are today. Each team member should have a clear understanding of their respective role and of the process across a timeline.

*In order to properly understand the big picture,*
*everyone should fear becoming mentally clouded and*
*obsessed with one small section of truth.*
XUN KUANG

For every engagement, lay out the steps from the finishing point back to the starting point.

Assign timelines to the process so that the appropriate amount of time is spent on each step.

_____

_____

_____

_____

_____

_____

_____

*We often plough so much energy into the big picture, we forget the pixels.*
SILVIA CARTWRIGHT

# Be Confident, but Not Arrogant

*Act as if it were impossible to fail.*
DOROTHEA BRANDE

There's a fine line between confidence and arrogance. The former is attractive and pulls teams together. The latter is a demotivator. The best way to distinguish between the two is to understand that confident professionals believe in their ability to figure things out on their own or with the help of others, and arrogant persons conduct themselves as if they have all the answers—they exhibit the "smartest guy in the room" syndrome.

*If you are knocked down, you can't lose your guts.*
*You need to play with supreme confidence, or you'll lose again,*
*and then losing becomes a habit.*
JOE PATERNO

In your opinion, which partners in your firm consistently conduct themselves with confidence?

_____

_____

What behaviors do they exhibit? Mimic those behaviors.

_____

_____

Which partners do you feel are arrogant? Don't behave like them.

_____

*I'm not arrogant. I just believe there's no human problem*
*that couldn't be solved—if people would simply do as I tell 'em.*
DONALD REGAN

# Keep Your Ego in Check

*Ego, that great motor which drives men to accomplishment,*
*but also injures their perspective so they imagine themselves*
*suns around which all other events orbit.*
LEWIS NIZER

A healthy ego is the cornerstone of a successful attorney. You need one to lead an engagement and represent a client. The trick is to not let your ego become overinflated. In such a case, in the attorney's mind everything is about him or her and this person has lost their way professionally.

*The most successful men are those who*
*recognize the ego in others, appreciate it, and take care of it.*
*Great men are simple and approachable and never*
*let their achievement or eminence keep them apart from those around.*
JOSEPH B. TRAINER

Ask your trusted teammates what they think of how you carry yourself with coworkers and with clients.

Make adjustments where consensus indicates improvements can be made.

_____

_____

_____

*Whenever I pick up a new book in my field, I am apt to turn first to the*
*index, and if I don't find my name there, I am likely to put it aside.*
CONFESSION OF A DISTINGUISHED IVY LEAGUE PROFESSOR
AND AUTHOR TO ALPHEUS THOMAS MASON,
OF PRINCETON UNIVERSITY, 1969,
CONFIRMED BY PROFESSOR MASON ON OCTOBER 8, 1969,
TO E. C. GERHART

## SELF-MANAGEMENT AND PERSONAL GROWTH

- ◆ Master Stress Management
- ◆ Adapt Easily to Changing Circumstances
- ◆ Maximize Use of Available Time
- ◆ Distinguish the Forest for the Trees
- ◆ Be Confident, but Not Arrogant
- ◆ Keep Your Ego in Check

# A Skilled Writer Is
# a Skilled Communicator

Simply put, being able to write well is the foundation for great communication. Until you master the art and the science of written communication, it is impossible to effectively inform, inspire, influence and collaborate with others. A firm's viability depends on its attorneys' communications. A client's first impression is often formed by their attorney's writing skills.

# When You Begin to Draft a Document, View the Blank Page As an Opportunity to Be Creative

*You can make anything by writing.*
C. S. LEWIS

Boilerplate language in documents is great because it improves efficiency. The trap is to fail to think beyond the boilerplate. Creative writing can paint a vivid picture that helps the reader better understand the message.

*A lawyer once said, "paper has a better memory than people,"*
*but the most important thing about the whole process is*
*what you put on the paper!*
EUGENE C. GERHART

Practice rewriting sentences and paragraphs into a more elegant form.

Write from different perspectives to reach the same conclusion.

---

---

---

---

---

---

*Writing is easy. All you do is sit staring at a blank sheet of paper*
*until the drops of blood form on your forehead.*
GENE FOWLER

# Don't Be Wedded to Your First Draft

*There is no such thing as good writing. There is only good rewriting.*
LEWIS D. BRANDEIS

The first draft is rarely, if ever, the best draft. It's simply the initial thoughts that create an outline. Almost without exception, the first draft needs refinement and polishing in subsequent drafts.

*Writing without revising is the literary equivalent of waltzing gaily out of the house in your underwear.*
PATRICIA FULLER

Make it a habit to read aloud the first draft and edit from there.

Elapsed time cleanses the mental palate. Editing is best, if you have the luxury, when at least 24 hours have elapsed since the first draft was written. Practice writing using this approach.

_____

_____

_____

_____

_____

_____

_____

_____

*The first draft is black and white. Editing gives the story color.*
EMMA HILL

# Draft with Precision and
# an Economy of Words

*So the writer who breeds more words than he needs,*
*is making a chore for the reader who reads.*
DR. SEUSS

Get to the point as quickly as possible and keep the number of topics to a minimum. If you "walk the reader around the block" writing about A to Z or go on and on about a single topic, you will lose the reader. A reader's attention span is not long. Make your point and cut out the fluff.

*A writer should have the precision of a poet and*
*the imagination of a scientist.*
VLADIMIR NABOKOV

During the editing process, pare down the verbiage and find more efficient ways to express the point and your meaning.

_____

_____

_____

_____

_____

_____

_____

_____

*To be brief is almost a condition of being inspired.*
GEORGE SANTAYANA

# Favor the Active Voice over the Passive Voice

*Learn to write. Never mind the damn statistics.*
*If you like statistics, become a CPA.*
JIM MURRAY

Writing in the active voice is less wordy, more direct and easier for the reader to understand. There's less ambiguity with the active voice and it creates a larger sense of urgency.

*[The active voice is the] vigorous voice, unashamed to say whodunit.*
*Passive voice is preferred by the weak, the cowardly,*
*ashamed to name the fink who told them what*
*they are evasively telling you.*
JOHN BREMNER

Recognize when you write actively (the dog bit the man) and passively (the man was bitten by the dog). During editing, find ways to convert the passive sentences to active ones.

Consider attending a writing seminar biannually.

---

*Verbs are the most important of all your tools.*
*They push the sentence forward and give it momentum.*
*Active verbs push hard; passive verbs tug fitfully.*
WILLIAM ZINSSER

43

# Eliminate Redundancy

*What's so tedious as a twice-told tale?*
HOMER

Make your point as forcefully as possible once and stop. When you start repeating yourself, you will lose the audience.

*Gobbledygook: talk or writing which is long, pompous,*
*vague, involved, usually with Latinized words.*
*It is also talk or writing which is merely long even though*
*the words are fairly simple, with repetition over and over again,*
*all of which could have been said in a few words.*
MAURY MAVERICK

Examine your writing for redundancy no matter how subtle. Eliminate the repetition.

_____

_____

_____

_____

_____

_____

_____

*What if one does say the same things—*
*of course in a little different form each time—*
*over and over? If he has anything to say worth saying,*
*that is just what he ought to do.*
OLIVER WENDELL HOLMES SR.

# Read *Plain English for Lawyers*
# by Richard Wydick

*The minute you read something you can't understand,*
*you can almost be sure it was drawn up by a lawyer.*
WILL ROGERS

There's a time and a place to write like an attorney. Know your audience. Communicate in a manner that is expected and easily understood. Clients aren't impressed with legalese.

*The question is how much potential ambiguity or misstatement*
*we should allow ourselves.*
GEORGE W. PIERCE

Buy the book and read it. List your top three takeaways. Follow them.

_____

_____

_____

_____

_____

_____

_____

_____

_____

*The words of law often look like words of the language you speak,*
*but when they are legal terms, they are not.*
DAVID BELLOS

# Keep Easy Access to Writing References

*Thought itself needs words. It runs on them like a ling wire,*
*and if it loses the habit of words, little by little it becomes shapeless, somber.*
UGO BETTI

Some variety in your vocabulary keeps things interesting. Using the same nouns, verbs, adjectives and adverbs gets old quickly for the reader. Spice things up with some variety. Dip into a writing reference book or a dictionary, thesaurus or legal dictionary to add flair to your writing.

*The use of words is to express ideas.*
*A perspicuity, therefore, requires not only that the ideas should*
*be distinctly formed, but they should be expressed*
*by words distinctly and exclusively appropriate to them.*
*But no language is so copious as to supply words and*
*phrases for every complex idea, or so correct as not to include many*
*equivocally denoting different ideas.*
JAMES MADISON

During the editing process, search for repetition of words. Find alternatives to eliminate unintended echoes.

Constantly strive to expand your vocabulary.

---

*Having imagination, it takes you an hour to write a paragraph that,*
*if you were unimaginative, would take you only a minute,*
*or you might not write the paragraph at all.*
FRANKLIN P. ADAMS

# Details, Details, Details

*A man does not know what he is saying until*
*he knows what he is not saying.*
G. K. CHESTERTON

A careless drafting could cost your client thousands of dollars—
and you, your reputation. During the editing process is when a
fresh set of eyes or another set of eyes is critical. Take your time
and think while editing. Read the sentences out loud. Pay close
attention to punctuation, especially the placement of commas.
And allow another critical thinker to also proofread your work.

*Michigan discovered in recent years,*
*that its state constitution inadvertently legalized slavery.*
*Section 8, Article 2 read:*
*"Neither slavery nor involuntary servitude,*
*unless for the punishment of crime, shall ever be tolerated in this state."*
*It was decided to shift the comma from its position*
*after "servitude" to a position after "slavery."*
THEODORE M. BERNSTEIN

Assign the responsibility for a second draft to the best proofreader
on the team.

_____

_____

_____

_____

*What is conceived well is expressed clearly.*
*And the words to say it with arrive with ease.*
NICOLAS BOILEAU-DESPRÉAUX

# Carefully Proofread Everything You Draft

*To be fully effective, speed must be coupled with accuracy.*
*Speed means nothing if the service rendered is not accurate.*
*Furthermore, accuracy must be present at all points.*
WILLIAM A. NIELANDER AND RAYMOND W. MILLER

Missing a simple mistake can undermine a great argument or change the economics of the agreement. Never rush through the proofreading process. It is nearly as important as the generation of the initial thoughts.

*Watch every detail that affects the accuracy of your work.*
ARTHUR C. NIELSEN

The more you proofread, the better you will become at it.

Proofread everything you write.

*Fast is fine, but accuracy is everything.*
WYATT EARP

# A SKILLED WRITER IS A SKILLED COMMUNICATOR

- When You Begin to Draft a Document, View the Blank Page As an Opportunity to Be Creative
- Don't Be Wedded to the First Draft
- Draft with Precision and an Economy of Words
- Favor the Active Voice over the Passive Voice
- Eliminate Redundancy
- Read *Plain English for Lawyers* by Richard Wydick
- Keep Easy Access to Writing References
- Details, Details, Details
- Carefully Proofread Everything You Draft

# A Matter of Ethics

Professional ethics are not an academic debate. Just one deviation from ethical behavior can arguably cause more damage to an attorney's reputation than all other professional shortcomings combined. Ethics violations are immediate career killers. Avoid the temptation to play interpretational games and dance along the razor's edge between right and wrong. It's your reputation. Your choices build it or destroy it. Use the following tools to make the right decisions.

# Always Take an Ethical Approach, Regardless of Its Impact on the Firm's Profitability

*Start with what is right rather than what is acceptable.*
PETER DRUCKER

Cutting corners by crossing an ethical line for a short-term gain never pays in the long run. Reputational damage to you and the firm can never be erased. The distraction as well as the cost of fighting the battle will likely last for years.

*There is no odor so bad as that which arises from goodness tainted.*
HENRY DAVID THOREAU

Always have a complete understanding of the ethical issues surrounding a matter that arises in your engagement.

Don't cross the line.

_____

_____

_____

_____

_____

_____

*First, there is the law. It must be obeyed.*
*But the law is the minimum. You must act ethically.*
IBM EMPLOYEE GUIDELINES

# It Takes Years of Hard Work, Dedication, Loyalty and Trust to Develop a Good Reputation and Only a Moment to Destroy It

*Character is much easier kept than recovered.*
THOMAS PAINE

Building a great reputation requires daily effort for decades. A great reputation is the condition precedent to the formation of trust between an attorney and his or her clients as well as all coworkers in the firm. Never take these facts for granted. All could be lost—never to return—in an instant if your ethical compass is lost.

*Reputation and learning are akin to capital assets,*
*like the goodwill of an old partnership. ...*
*For many, they are the only tools with which to hew*
*a pathway to success.*
BENJAMIN N. CARDOZO

Spend at least two hours a year reviewing the code of professional responsibilities.

_____

_____

_____

_____

*Character is a habit long continued.*
PLUTARCH

# It's Nearly Impossible to Get Rid of
# a Bad Reputation

*What people say behind your back is your standing in the community.*
EDGAR WATSON HOWE

Whether you're trying to land a new client, expand services for an existing one or lead your team on an engagement, your reputation is the first impression you make. Walking backwards while trying to defend or excuse a professional miscue is a fruitless exercise.

*Be it true or false, what is said about men often has*
*as much influence upon their lives, and especially upon*
*their destinies, as what they do.*
VICTOR HUGO

Just never go here. You will not be able to escape.

_____

_____

_____

_____

_____

_____

_____

_____

*It is generally much more shameful to lose a good reputation*
*than never to have acquired it.*
PLINY THE YOUNGER

# Don't Represent Clients Who Ask You to Deviate from the Code of Professional Responsibilities

*An important measure for keeping ourselves from wrong conduct,*
*therefore, is to keep ourselves in thought and action at a distance from it.*
GEORGE A. HALSEY

Your reputation is, in part, a reflection of the company you keep and the clients you represent. There is absolutely no upside to representing a client that encourages you to do something unethical. It will not end well if you do and don't be so naive to think this is the only time you will be asked to do so expressly or implicitly against your personal and professional code of ethics.

*Those who stand for nothing fall for anything.*
ALEXANDER HAMILTON

Be wary of the company you keep.

End your representation immediately in such a situation as when an ethical breach is requested. Full stop.

_____

_____

_____

_____

_____

*Did you expect the corporation to have a conscience,*
*when it has no soul to be damned, and no body to be kicked?*
EDWARD THURLOW

# A MATTER OF ETHICS

- Always Take an Ethical Approach, Regardless of Its Impact on the Firm's Profitability
- It Takes Years of Hard Work, Dedication, Loyalty and Trust to Build a Good Reputation and Only a Moment to Destroy It
- It's Nearly Impossible to Get Rid of a Bad Reputation
- Don't Represent Clients Who Ask You to Deviate from the Code of Professional Responsibilities

# LEGAL SKILLS

Many legal skills are not self-evident. The legal skills discussed here transcend your knowledge of substantive law and cannot be learned from reading them in a book. Like the sport of golf, they must be practiced repetitively so you develop the proper feel for when to use them in a given situation. Some require you to adapt to the surrounding environment. Others require you to create the environment. Your ability to understand what the setting requires and take the lead to make what is needed happen will determine your success.

# A Day in the Life of a Lawyer

L et's set the actual practice of law aside for a moment and consider that a proficient attorney must adapt to unfamiliar environments. You must keep your ego in check. When a client is in need, it doesn't matter what time of the day or day of the week it is—you're on call. Often, you'll find yourself operating in uncertain environments, and decisiveness is required when it is not obvious what to do. And remember, as discussed previously, the practice of law is a team sport. As an attorney, you will always be challenged to bring out the best in your team.

# Adapt to the Uncertainty That Permeates the Practice of Law

*It is always probable that something improbable will happen.*
LOGAN E. BLECKLEY

Very few things in life are black and white. Nearly everything in the practice of law is gray, and there are many shades. Find comfort in the ebbs and flows of an engagement. It may feel like a roller-coaster ride at times, but this is the world you will operate in throughout your career.

*The power of the lawyer is in the uncertainty of the law.*
JEREMY BENTHAM

How do you emotionally react to surprises? Identify how you can retract much of the emotion from a situation.

How do you find certainty in fluid circumstances?

<br>
<br>
<br>
<br>
<br>
<br>
<br>

*A little uncertainty is good for everything.*
HENRY KISSINGER

# Lawyers Are No Different from Plumbers: Both Are on Call 24/7

*(Law) is not a profession at all, but rather a business service*
*station and repair shop.*
ADLAI E. STEVENSON

When a client is in need, not much thought is given to the impact this has on their attorney. The client–attorney relationship is one-way: it's all about the client and their needs. But if you don't set parameters with your clients, there won't be any. It behooves you to do so at the start of an engagement.

*A professional is a man who can do his best at a time*
*when he doesn't particularly feel like it.*
ALISTAIR COOKE

Do you have a policy in place with clients regarding your personal time? If not, what did you learn?

_____

_____

_____

_____

List below the boundaries you will set with future clients.

_____

_____

_____

*Either you run the day or the day runs you.*
JIM ROHN

# Start Your Day As Early As Possible

*In the morning a man walks with his whole body;*
*in the evening, only his legs.*
RALPH WALDO EMERSON

The best way to increase your work product efficiency is to start work early in the day because then you will experience fewer interruptions. The easier drive or ride in to a quiet office also provides for a better frame of mind for thinking and decision-making. Take advantage of mornings.

*Lose an hour in the morning, and you will be all day hunting for it.*
RICHARD WHATELY

Adjust your nighttime routine so you get enough sleep and can arrive at the office at 7:00 a.m. daily.

_____

_____

_____

_____

_____

_____

_____

_____

_____

*The morning is wiser than the evening.*
RUSSIAN PROVERB

# Be Decisive

*Make every decision as if you own the whole company.*
ROBERT TOWNSEND

Nothing frustrates a client more than a wishy-washy attorney. Clients don't want to hear "on the other hand..." Make decisions, recommend an option, and inform clients of the risks. If they are uncomfortable with the risk, you can present a second option. You can't "pick your horse" after it crosses the finish line.

*If I had to sum up in one word what makes a good manager,*
*I'd say decisiveness.*
*You can use the fanciest computers to gather the numbers,*
*but in the end, you have to set a timetable and act.*
*I don't mean rashly.*
*I am sometimes described as a flamboyant leader and*
*a hip-shooter, a fly-by-the-seat-of-the-pants operator.*
*But if that were true, I could have never been successful in the business.*
LEE IACOCCA

Continually practice gathering as much information as possible before making a decision.

Before deciding, look at the issue from a different perspective and try to poke holes in your initial decision to determine its viability.

_____

_____

_____

*You'll never have all the information you need to make a decision.*
*If you did, it would be a foregone conclusion, not a decision.*
DAVID J. MAHONEY JR.

# Maximize Your Use of the Support Staff

The support staff is the backbone of the operation. They can make or break the engagement. Training, communication and situational awareness are key elements for the team's success.

Does the entire team have the project plan for the engagement?

Does each member of your team understand their responsibilities in the engagement?

Have you scheduled status report/update meetings?

# Proper Supervision and Periodic Evaluation of the Support Staff Will Increase Productivity Tremendously

*Treat people as if they were what they ought to be and you help them become what they are capable of being.*
JOHANN WOLFGANG VON GOETHE

People need to know where they stand and how they can improve. They also need to be recognized for their contributions. Provide continuous and consistent feedback to your team. Feedback need not, and should not, always be given in a formal setting.

*To succeed ... you need to find something to hold on to, something to motivate you, something to inspire you.*
TONY DORSETT

Set annual reviews for your teammates. Where improvement is needed, provide clear direction of what is expected.

Give praise and compliments in real time.

_____

_____

_____

_____

_____

_____

*People ask you for criticism, but they only want praise.*
W. SOMERSET MAUGHAM

# Never Take the Support Staff for Granted

*Few great men could pass personnel.*
PAUL GOODMAN

Far too many attorneys treat support staff disrespectfully, primarily because staff don't have a law degree. Don't fall into the trap of treating support staff as second-class citizens. They can make or break your performance. The hardest way to learn their value is to lose them.

*Appreciate everything your associates do for the business.*
*Nothing else can quite substitute for a few well-chosen,*
*well-timed sincere words of praise.*
*They're absolutely free and worth a fortune.*
SAM WALTON

Make it a point to thank and praise each member of your support staff on a weekly basis.

_____

_____

_____

_____

_____

_____

_____

*Treat employees like partners, and they act like partners.*
FRED ALLEN

# A DAY IN THE LIFE OF A LAWYER

- Adapt to the Uncertainty That Permeates the Practice of Law
- Lawyers Are No Different from Plumbers: Both are on Call 24/7
- Start Your Day As Early As Possible
- Be Decisive
- Maximize Your Use of the Support Staff
- Proper Supervision and Periodic Evaluation of the Support Staff Will Increase Productivity Tremendously
- Never Take the Support Staff for Granted

# Above and Beyond

One of the biggest challenges for an attorney is the absence of a tangible deliverable. A client's perception of value is based on their initial expectations, so be sure to set reasonable expectations at the start of the engagement and then find ways throughout to add more value than what's expected. Understand that adding value is rarely achieved with a single act or event. It's usually accomplished by the aggregation of many actions over time.

# Don't Be Just a Problem Solver.
# Be a Value Adder Too

*Problems are only opportunities in work clothes.*
HENRY J. KAISER

Having a clear understanding of the client's needs and business is critical. As you navigate the engagement, search for opportunities to capture that are meaningful for the client. This is the purist form of exceeding expectations and adding value beyond achieving an agreed-upon legal engagement.

*Human service is the highest form of self-interest for the person who serves.*
ELBERT HUBBARD

How well do you know your client's business?

_____

_____

What's most important to your client?

_____

_____

If the answer to the first question is "not very well" and you are not 100 percent sure about the answer to the second question, you have some work to do.

_____

_____

*We are thankful for good-will rather than for services,*
*for the motive than the quantum of favour received.*
WILLIAM HAZLITT

# When Counseling Clients,
# Draw on the Vast Experiences of
# the Other Attorneys in Your Firm

*We think that the strongest logic is that of experience.*
BENJAMIN GRAHAM

No one attorney has all the answers and there is no substitute for experience, especially when drawn from the experience of many. Take advantage of this resource. Again, the practice of law is a team sport. Tap into your team.

*To an imagination of any scope the most far-reaching form of power is not money, it is the command of ideas.*
OLIVER WENDELL HOLMES JR.

How well do you know the expertise of your firm's attorneys? Pay close attention to the matters they serve.

_____

_____

Seek input on the engagement you serve from the right attorneys.

_____

_____

_____

_____

_____

*Upon this point a page of history is worth a volume of logic.*
OLIVER WENDELL HOLMES JR.

# Don't Simply Conclude That
# a Particular Approach Will Fail
# without Providing Alternatives

*Well, I don't know as I want a lawyer to tell me what I cannot do.*
*I hired him to tell me how to do what I want to do.*
JOHN PIERPANT MORGAN

There is almost always a Plan B. Moreover, it may make sense to attack an issue from more than one angle. It is imprudent to approach a matter single mindedly. Strive to find alternative approaches and provide choices to your client. Unpleasant surprises occur on occasion. The absence of other options will likely leave you and your client in an unenviable position.

*Have a Plan B, and maybe even a Plan C.*
*Because unexpected changes are most difficult to handle*
*when we don't have a backup.*
GERMANY KENT

Push yourself and your team to create alternative paths to the desired outcome.

Always be prepared for an unexpected twist.

---

*Some men go through a forest and see no firewood.*
ENGLISH PROVERB

# Develop a Working Vocabulary and Understanding in Several Fields

*Don't rely on a single discipline—no one specialist has the entire answer.*
JAMES VOTRUBA

Issues don't occur in silos; legal matters are not single subject. It's imperative that you can at least sense that there are other fields of law that can or might impact the issue at hand. This awareness enables you to reach out to the right expertise in the firm for assistance.

*The illiterate of the 21st Century will not be those who cannot read and write, but those who cannot learn, unlearn, and relearn.*
ALVIN TOFFLER

Attend other monthly or quarterly practice group meetings. Absorb the discussions around current issues.

Take a basic one- or two-hour continuing legal education (CLE) course outside your practice area once a year.

_____

_____

_____

_____

_____

*If the only tool you have is a hammer,*
*you tend to see every problem as a nail.*
ABRAHAM MASLOW

# Stay on Top of Current Developments
# in Your Field

*The school is not the end but only the beginning of an education.*
CALVIN COOLIDGE

The evolution of law began hundreds of years ago, and it will never stop. As changes occur in society, the law evolves to try to keep pace. As a result, the burden is on the attorney to stay current and not be caught off guard.

*Nature without learning is blind, learning apart from nature is fractional, and practice in the absence of both is aimless.*
PLUTARCH

Stay abreast of changes through legal periodicals and podcasts and your bar association memberships.

Make it a habit to attend your firm's monthly practice group meetings, where changes in the law are often presented.

Attend CLE courses that specifically address the latest changes in the law.

_____

_____

_____

_____

_____

*The great difficulty in education is to get experience out of ideas.*
GEORGE SANTAYANA

## ABOVE AND BEYOND

- Don't Be Just a Problem Solver. Be a Value Adder Too
- When Counseling Clients, Draw on the Vast Experiences of the Other Attorneys in Your Firm
- Don't Simply Conclude That a Particular Approach Will Fail without Providing Alternatives
- Develop a Working Vocabulary and Understanding in Several Fields
- Stay on Top of Current Developments in Your Field

# Client Care

The client's interests come first. As their attorney, you have a duty to act in their best interest. To do so, a proper mindset, attitude, approach and planning are prerequisites the vast majority of which can't be taught in a classroom. You learn these essentials from experience and/or by observing mentors.

# It's Better to Ask Than to Assume

*Assumption is the mother of screw-up.*
ANGELO DONGHIA

Lawyers should only operate in a world of facts. To rely on anything short of verified facts is foolish and irresponsible.

*I think that one of the principal rules for a lawyer is that you should never*
*assume anything, even if your own client tells it to you.*
*You should always go out and get the best proof you can find on the issue.*
*In most instances it will corroborate what your client has said.*
*But in some instances, it may cast doubt on what he's saying,*
*or suggest other lines of inquiry.*
*There simply is no substitute for being thorough.*
J. EDWARD LUMBARD

Verify everything that you are relying on for a legal position.

Never take someone's word or rely on verbal statements. Everything should be in writing, and even then, other written corroboration may be needed.

---

---

---

---

---

---

---

*Unverified assumptions cause more errors than wrong reasoning.*
EUGENE C. GERHART

# Understand and Define the Issues at Hand

*A problem well stated is a problem half solved.*
CHARLES F. KETTERING

If you can't see the issue or the problem, how will you find the solution? Don't put the cart before the horse when attacking an issue. Before entertaining a thought regarding the solution, make sure you have a thorough understanding of the problem.

*First settle what the case is, before you argue it.*
LORD CHIEF JUSTICE HOWE

After meeting with a client and performing cursory research, spend time discussing and defining the issues and problems with fellow attorneys in the firm.

_____

_____

_____

_____

_____

_____

_____

_____

_____

*If you are able to state a problem—any problem—and if it is important*
*enough, then the problem can be solved.*
EDWIN LAND

# You Can't Listen Very Well
# If You Don't Stop Talking

*A good listener is not only popular everywhere,*
*but after a while he knows something.*
WILLIAM MIZNER

To thoroughly understand all of the issues presented by your client, you must listen closely. The ability to ask great questions to learn more information is a must as well. The worst thing an attorney can do is prematurely pontificate on the solution. The better you are as a listener, the less likely this will occur.

*Long-windedness is one of the shortcomings of*
*modern formal communication.*
*Although the lawyer is not the only or the worst offender, he has his own*
*built-in kind of proliferation in an occupation*
*which stands in need of the succinctly accurate statement.*
*One must learn somehow to state the vital issues simply and then stop.*
FRANCIS BERGAN

Practice listening closely without interrupting or drawing conclusions prematurely.

Learn to ask pointed questions to uncover subtleties.

*Everything has been said already;*
*but as no one listens, we must always begin again.*
ANDRÉ GIDE

# Be Sensitive to Your Clients' Aversity to Risk

*Tact in audacity is knowing how far you can go without going too far.*
JEAN COCTEAU

Not every client has the stomach or financial wherewithal to achieve an impressive victory. Discuss a variety of solutions to your client's legal problem and know your client's comfort level with each approach. Do this early in the engagement so there is a mutual understanding of the risks involved with the chosen strategy.

> *People wish to be settled:*
> *only as far as they are unsettled is there*
> *any hope for them.*
> RALPH WALDO EMERSON

Carefully and concisely explain to your client the risks involved with the strategies that you will employ in the engagement.

Have the client reflect back their understanding of your explanation.

Confirm the conversation and agreement of strategy in writing.

_____

_____

_____

_____

> *I also am not particularly risk-averse—*
> *I don't mind jumping off a cliff If I trust the people*
> *who've told me they'll catch me at the bottom.*
> JEFF VANDERMEER

# Be Aggressive, but Not Confrontational

*A gentleman is a man who can disagree without being disagreeable.*
H. L. MENCKEN

It's one thing to represent your client with passion and another to be abrasive for the sake of making life difficult for opposing counsel. The latter will likely end in a toxic environment where compromise cannot be had in the future. Opposing counsel will not tolerate disrespectful behavior. Remember, paybacks can be a bitch.

*Don't take the wrong side of an argument just because*
*your opponent has taken the right side.*
BALTASAR GRACIÁN

Before going on the attack, ask yourself how much of your ferocity is driven by emotion and what your endgame is.

Moreover, ask yourself how you would receive or react to the aggressive approach and argument you are about to employ.

_____

_____

_____

_____

_____

_____

_____

*Most quarrels amplify a misunderstanding.*
ANDRÉ GIDE

# Properly Staff Clients' Matters

*Hire the best people and then delegate.*
CAROL A. TABER

Again, the practice of law is a team sport. Putting your best foot forward should be the case right out of the gate. After you have properly identified and defined the issues, assign the appropriate experts and support staff on day one. Adding personnel midstream is inefficient and may cause errors to occur.

*The important thing to recognize is that it takes a team,*
*and the team ought to get credit for the wins and the losses.*
*Successes have many fathers, failures have none.*
PHILIP CALDWELL

Do you have the right players on the team for the engagement?

_____

_____

Do they have sufficient resources?

_____

_____

_____

Will they be spread too thin?

_____

_____

_____

*Soldiers win battles and generals get the credit.*
NAPOLEON BONAPARTE

# Never Underestimate Your Client or Opposing Counsel

*A man surprised is half beaten.*
THOMAS FULLER

Unless it's your birthday, surprises aren't good. You need to approach every engagement fully prepared. It doesn't matter whether most of the facts or the law are on your side or that your firm has the better reputation—there are no sure things in this world. Never forget that David defeated Goliath.

*To see a man beaten not by a better opponent but by himself is a tragedy.*
CUS D'AMATO

Have you and your team thoroughly listed all of the possible counterarguments?

_____

_____

_____

Are you prepared for each of them?

_____

_____

_____

_____

*I never underestimate my opponent, but I never underestimate my talents.*
HALE IRWIN

# Know When to Let Your Clients Negotiate the Deal

*As is our confidence, so is our capacity.*
WILLIAM HAZLITT

Once the lawyers get involved, a matter takes on the aura of confrontation. There's no getting around that fact. It's human nature. At times, clients should verbally negotiate a transaction as far as possible because they better understand the business aspect of the transaction and there is usually some level of trust between the parties on which advancement can be achieved.

*Successful negotiation is not about getting to "yes";*
*it's about mastering "no" and understanding what the path*
*to an agreement is.*
CHRISTOPHER VOSS

In non-adversarial situations, encourage clients to negotiate as much of the deal as possible. It will speed up the transaction and reduce the legal fees.

_____

_____

_____

_____

_____

_____

*The most critical thing in a negotiation is to get inside your opponent's head*
*and figure out what he really wants.*
JACOB LEW

## CLIENT CARE

- It's Better to Ask Than to Assume

- Understand and Define the Issues at Hand

- You Can't Listen Very Well If You Don't Stop Talking

- Be Sensitive to Your Clients' Aversity to Risk

- Be Aggressive, but Not Confrontational

- Properly Staff Clients' Matters

- Never Underestimate Your Client or Opposing Counsel

- Know When to Let Your Clients Negotiate the Deal

# Open to Negotiations

A "born negotiator" is a myth. Rather, you need to learn a variety of skills drawn from various disciplines to reach agreements that are beneficial to all parties. As with any sport, you cannot learn how to negotiate by reading a book. It involves a great deal of practice. That is why I have provided you with inspiration and instructions on how to get out there and apply negotiation skills in the real world. Once mastered, they will help you to achieve sustainable value and reduce conflict. Skill in negotiation is essential for the execution of a well-planned strategy.

# Never Draw Conclusions Until You Have Gathered All the Facts and Defined the Issues

*To live effectively is to live with adequate information.*
NORBERT WIENER

The older we get, the more often we think, "I've seen this movie," believing we know how the situation will transpire. Most times we are correct, but not always. The practice of law is not a game of horseshoes where being close is good enough. Follow the process by gathering and verifying the facts, properly defining the issues and then working on solving the problem.

*Experience seems to most of us to lead to conclusions,*
*but empiricism has sworn never to draw them.*
GEORGE SANTAYANA

Whenever you start jumping to conclusions, catch yourself and stop.

Follow the assignments set forth earlier in the first three skills in the "Client Care" section.

---

*Life is the art of drawing sufficient conclusions from insufficient premises.*
SAMUEL BUTLER

# Address One Issue at a Time

*If you choose two rabbits, both will escape.*
ANONYMOUS

The most effective way to achieve multiple outcomes is to address issues in a sequential process. It's always best to resolve issues individually rather than collectively. When there's too many balls in the air, things become confusing, priorities are lost and very little is accomplished. If you ever get the chance to participate in the negotiation of a collective bargaining agreement, you will quickly learn the importance of prioritizing issues.

*It is best to do things systematically, since we are only human,*
*and disorder is our worst enemy.*
HESIOD

Identify all of the issues in the engagement.

Prioritize them.

Resolve each one in an orderly manner. Try to avoid tabling any without resolution or agreement before advancing to the next.

_____

_____

_____

_____

_____

*The mightiest rivers lose their force when split up into several streams.*
OVID

# Have Patience

*In the university they don't tell you that the greater part of the law is*
*learning to tolerate fools.*
DORIS LESSING

When you lose patience, you're often overcome with emotion. The best mindset for the legal profession is one devoid of emotion. Life does not always happen at the speed or in the manner we want in the moment. Don't let setbacks affect you. Stay in control of your emotions and keep advancing the strategy to reach the desired outcome.

*If you are strong and a giant,*
*it doesn't mean that you react like a weak person.*
*Patience is a character of a strong man.*
*It is not the character of a weak man.*
SHEIKH ZAKI YAMANI

Instead of burning energy reacting to a setback, redirect your efforts to finding ways to get the strategy back on track.

Accept the fact that events don't always go as initially planned.

Be intentional in your ability not to let circumstances frustrate you.

---

---

---

---

*In negotiation, he who cares less, wins.*
ANONYMOUS

# Don't Lose Your Temper

*The vehemence of a man's emotions is no proof that*
*his opinion is right.*
EUGENE C. GERHART

Everybody gets upset from time to time. That's perfectly normal. But allowing your anger to cause a change in strategy in the form of a knee-jerk reaction is foolish. Emotions should never dictate or alter strategy because that's a recipe for disaster. If you're upset, find a colleague to vent your feelings with and then return to problem-solving.

*Be calm in arguing; for fierceness makes error a fault,*
*and truth discourtesy.*
GEORGE HERBERT

What actions do you take to diffuse your anger?

_____

_____

_____

Find a colleague you can vent feelings to and discuss whether a rational reaction is more appropriate.

_____

_____

_____

*Anger can be an effective negotiating tool,*
*but only as a calculated act, never as a reaction.*
MARK MCCORMACK

# A Point or Two Can Be Made with Silence

*Silence is one of the hardest arguments to refute.*
JOSH BILLINGS

Here's the easiest way to make a point and cause opposing counsel to feel incredibly uncomfortable after you drop the mic: Answer a question or make a final assertion and then stop talking. Just stare into the opposing counsel's eyes. Do not speak until after he or she does. Allow them to finish their rebuttal and then go right back to staring until they ask if you have anything to say. Reply no, and move on. Point, set, match.

*The Power of Silence.*
*If there is one pragmatic—and often most difficult—*
*shill in the art of negotiating, it is learning to be silent.*
*A really skilled negotiator knows the power of silence.*
*It frequently leads the other party to say more than*
*he should or to move off of position to more reasonable*
*(i.e., more acceptable to you) position.*
ARTHUR J. SABIN

Practice the power of silence when the opportunity presents itself.

*Wise men say nothing in dangerous times.*
JOHN SELDEN

# Know When to Shift Gears and Take a Different Approach

*We often get in quicker by the back door than by the front.*
NAPOLEON BONAPARTE

Banging your head against the wall or pounding your fist on the table gets painful after a while. Sheer force does not change people's minds or achieve a desired outcome. Instead, a well-designed tactic must always be employed.

*If there are obstacles, the shortest line between*
*two points may be the crooked line.*
BERTOLT BRECHT

Ask yourself what's not working.

Dig deep to identify the shortcoming or resistance.

Brainstorm with the team to develop an alternative approach.

_____

_____

_____

_____

_____

_____

*Firmness in support of fundamentals, with flexibility and tactics and*
*method, is the key to any hope of progress in negotiation.*
DWIGHT D. EISENHOWER

# A Compromise Is Often Better
# Than Litigation

*Agree, for the law is costly.*
WILLIAM CAMDEN

Litigation is expensive and it's never quick. It's emotionally drain-
ing and a distraction to your client. Moreover, the results are never
guaranteed, no matter how promising the facts appear. Compromise in the short term does not always feel great, but it's much
better than having your client spend a ton of money and end up
in the same place or worse.

*A lean compromise is better than a fat lawsuit.*
GEORGE HERBERT

Before going on an all-out attack, explore all avenues to reach a
settlement.

<br><br><br><br><br><br>

*When there's a rift in the loot,*
*the business of a lawyer is to widen the rift and gather the loot.*
ARTHUR GARFIELD HAYS

# Initially Ask for More Than You Expect. Conversely, Initially Offer Less Than You Expect to Pay

*Yield to all and you will soon have nothing to yield.*
AESOP

First asking for more or offering less is an approach that may be fundamental and self-evident, but it bears reminding. Initial offers are never accepted. More times than not, second and third offers are countered with intensity. As a result, leave room between the start point and the end point that can be justified.

*Don't bargain yourself down before you get to the table.*
CAROL FROHLINGER

In the planning stages, identify the desired outcome and work back to where the economics are today.

Develop supporting arguments (for and against) for each round of offers.

_____

_____

_____

_____

_____

_____

*"Let us agree not to step on each other's feet," said the cock to the horse.*
ENGLISH PROVERB

# Practice Is the Best Education

*A man who carries a cat by the tail learns something*
*he can learn in no other way.*
MARK TWAIN

Role-playing is an excellent exercise to prepare for negotiation. Having a formidable colleague challenge your position and tactics beforehand will not only strengthen your skills but also raise issues and arguments that you did not consider. Practicing negotiating also helps you refine your response to the resistance you expect.

*The more you practice the better you get,*
*the more freedom you have to create.*
JOCKO WILLINK

Role-play—or at a minimum have a spirited discussion with a colleague—before going to the negotiation table.

_____

_____

_____

_____

_____

_____

_____

*The more I practice, the luckier I get.*
GARY PLAYER

## OPEN TO NEGOTIATIONS

- Never Draw Conclusions Until You Have Gathered All the Facts and Defined the Issues
- Address One Issue at a Time
- Have Patience
- Don't Lose Your Temper
- A Point or Two Can Be Made with Silence
- Know When to Shift Gears and Take a Different Approach
- A Compromise Is Often Better Than Litigation
- Initially Ask for More Than You Expect. Conversely, Initially Offer Less Than You Expect to Pay
- Practice Is the Best Education

# In the Face of Opposition

This may sound a bit counterintuitive, but it's in your best interest to be nice to opposing counsel. Although they may be your adversary, they are not your enemy. How you treat them is a reflection of your character and it affects your reputation. Strategically, having a healthy, respectful relationship with the opposition during the engagement will likely serve you well in reaching the final outcome because, in the end, on some level, you may need their cooperation.

# Know Opposing Counsel's Strengths and Weaknesses

*You can discover what your enemy fears most by observing*
*the means he uses to frighten you.*
ERIC HOFFER

Who are you up against? How much experience does he or she have in these types of engagements? What do you know about opposing counsel's firm?

*The idea is not to block every shot.*
*The idea is to make your opponent believe that*
*you might block every shot.*
BILL RUSSELL

Do your research on LinkedIn and the opposing counsel's website.

_____

_____

_____

_____

Poll attorneys in your firm to aggregate personal experiences regarding opposing counsel.

_____

_____

_____

*The fellow that agrees with everything you say is either a fool or*
*he is getting ready to skin you.*
FRANK MCKINNEY HUBBARD

# Praise Your Opposing Counsel More Than They Deserve without Being Disrespectful

*Every cock is proud of his own dunghill.*
THOMAS FULLER

Lawyers often have overinflated egos. Play to it when you see it. Reinforce opposing counsel's thought that they are the center of the universe. This simple tactic can distract your opponent. It may create the opening you need to succeed.

*Our ego is our silent partner—too often with a controlling interest.*
CULLEN HIGHTOWER

Go for it when the opportunity presents itself!

_____

_____

_____

_____

_____

_____

_____

_____

_____

*Egotism is the anesthetic that dulls the pain of stupidity.*
FRANK LEAHY

# Be Courteous with Opposing Counsel, But Don't Let Your Guard Down

*All doors open to courtesy.*
THOMAS FULLER

All engagements are emotionally charged on some level. There's no need to amp them up. There is no upside to being rude or condescending. If anything, it's best to diffuse the potentially negative emotion whenever possible. There's a high probability that you will need opposing counsel's cooperation at some point. Treating them with respect beforehand will go a long way.

*The mere fact that an approach is gentlemanly does not mean it is weak.*
LAWRENCE H. COOKE

Be situationally aware of how the manner in which you communicate and the tactics you employ affect the emotions of opposing counsel.

*The greater the man the greater the courtesy.*
ALFRED, LORD TENNYSON

# Don't Play Petty Games
# with Opposing Counsel

*One has to try to strike the jugular and let the rest go.*
OLIVER WENDELL HOLMES JR.

Playing games is a waste of everyone's time and it reflects poorly on your character and hurts your reputation. Always be the bigger person.

*Small things make base men proud.*
SHAKESPEARE

Don't go here no matter how tempting.

_____

_____

_____

_____

_____

_____

_____

_____

_____

_____

_____

_____

*Don't play games if you can't afford to lose.*
GERMANY KENT

# Never Put Opposing Counsel in a Position
# Where They Can't Save Face

*Never insult an alligator until you have crossed the river.*
CORDELL HULL

Pigs get fat, hogs get slaughtered. Don't be greedy. Opposing counsel needs to walk away with some kind of victory no matter how small.

*An injured friend is the bitterest of foes.*
THOMAS JEFFERSON

Don't be a hog.

*You must never try to make all the money that's in the deal.*
*Let the other fellow make some money too,*
*because if you have a reputation for always making all the money,*
*you won't have many deals.*
J. PAUL GETTY

## IN THE FACE OF OPPOSITION

◆ Know Opposing Counsel's Strengths and Weaknesses

◆ Praise Your Opposing Counsel More Than They Deserve without Being Disrespectful

◆ Be Courteous with Opposing Counsel, but Don't Let Your Guard Down

◆ Don't Play Petty Games with Opposing Counsel

◆ Never Put Opposing Counsel in a Position Where They Can't Save Face

# Team Spirit

The success of a team, and your standing within the team, comes down to communication. Whether it's keeping others apprised or challenging the strength of a position, the quality of the communication will have a big impact on the outcome. Your advancement in the firm is contingent on the communication you project internally about your capabilities and the communication between you and your mentor.

# Know the Expertise of Each Professional at Your Firm

*Alone we can do so little; together we can do so much.*
HELEN KELLER

Regardless of the size of your firm, you are surrounded by expertise and decades of experience. Tap into it and make use of all available resources. To do so, you need to know who on the team brings what to the table. Reading attorney bios is a great start. Having conversations is even better.

*The key thing that makes national law firms work is synergy; with the right combinations, one and one can make three.*
STEVEN KUMBLE

Network constantly within your firm.

Get to know as many of the attorneys as possible and have them get to know you.

_____

_____

_____

_____

_____

_____

_____

*Individually we are one drop; but together we are an ocean.*
RYUNOSUKE SATORO

# Find a Mentor

*Give a man a fish, and you feed him for a day.*
*Teach a man to fish, and you feed him for a lifetime.*
CHINESE PROVERB

Nothing will accelerate your career more than a mentor. They will kickstart your professional development, assist in goal setting, hold you accountable, help you develop leadership skills, raise your confidence and open doors for you.

*A mentor is someone with a willingness to help others,*
*who has a capacity to inspire, a determination to work hard,*
*a clear sense of vision, an inspiring purpose,*
*a deep sense of integrity and an appreciation for joy.*
KERRY KENNEDY

If your firm did not assign a mentor to you, go find one today.

_____

_____

_____

_____

_____

_____

_____

*If you cannot see where you are going,*
*ask someone who has been there before.*
J. LOREN NORRIS

# When Resolving Issues, Bounce Ideas off Other Attorneys

*The law is not the place of the artist or the poet.*
*The law is the calling of thinkers.*
OLIVER WENDELL HOLMES JR.

Nobody has all of the answers, and often initial strategies and responses need refinement. The best way to discover better answers or to refine your thoughts is to seek others' input or critique. Put ideas to the test before they are put into practice.

*The secret of business is to know something that nobody else knows.*
ARISTOTLE ONASSIS

Make it a habit of putting ideas and strategies to the test with colleagues before you put them into use.

_____

_____

_____

_____

_____

_____

_____

_____

*Results? Why, man, I have gotten a lot of results.*
*I know 50,000 things that won't work.*
THOMAS EDISON

# Keep Your Teammates Informed of Where Things Stand at All Times

*Coming together is a beginning; keeping together is progress;*
*working together is success.*
EDWARD EVERETT HALE

There are few things more embarrassing than when the right hand doesn't know what the left hand is doing. When a team is well-informed, it operates efficiently and effectively. Errors are reduced. Great communication is a reflection of a well-run operation. Clients appreciate and value excellent cross communication during an engagement.

*More information is always better than less.*
*When people know the reason things are happening,*
*even if it is bad news,*
*they can adjust their expectations and react accordingly.*
*Keeping people in the dark only serves to stir negative emotions.*
SIMON SINEK

Implement procedures that ensure that all teammates are kept up-to-date on all matters in the engagement at all times.

Alerts should be sent when new developments arise.

_____

_____

_____

_____

*In teamwork, silence isn't golden, it's deadly.*
MARK SANBORN

# Market Your Skills to
# the Professionals of Your Firm

*Man does not only sell commodities,*
*he sells himself and feels himself to be a commodity.*
ERICH FROMM

Never underestimate the importance of internal marketing. Don't be shy about building your personal brand with your colleagues. Whenever possible, take the opportunity to demonstrate your capabilities and accomplishments. It's your responsibility to be your own advocate and get people talking about you, in short, word of mouth.

*Doing business without advertising is like winking at a girl in the dark.*
*You know what you are doing, but nobody else does.*
STEUART HENDERSON BRITT

Volunteer to write blogs or internal memos on recent changes in the law.

Speak at monthly practice group meetings.

---

---

---

---

*On average 8 out of 10 people will read your headline copy,*
*but 2 out of 10 will read the rest.*
BRIAN CLARK

## TEAM SPIRIT

- Know the Expertise of Each Professional at Your Firm
- Find a Mentor
- When Resolving Issues, Bounce Ideas off Other Attorneys
- Keep Your Teammates Informed of Where Things Stand at All Times
- Market Your Skills to the Professionals of Your Firm

# Leading the Pack

Your leadership skills, probably more than any others, bring out the best in your teammates and in you. Equally important, you can use your leadership skills to create a fun working environment. They are at the core of the relationships you possess with your coworkers and clients. How you comport yourself as a leader demonstrates the respect you have for clients and colleagues because it reflects your priorities.

# Strive to Become an Expert in a Field

*Knowledge is a process of piling up facts; wisdom lies in their simplification.*
MARTIN H. FISCHER

Being a jack-of-all-trades, master of none is not a great career strategy in the practice of law. Whether you are the billing attorney or the managing attorney for an engagement, you must be completely immersed in a specific area. That must be brought to the table for your clients and your teams.

*Reputation and learning are akin to capital assets,*
*like the goodwill of an old partnership.*
*... For many, they are the only tools with which to hew a pathway to success.*
*The money spent in acquiring them is well and wisely spent.*
BENJAMIN N. CARDOZO

Find your passion for a specific area of law. Passion arises where intellectual curiosity resides.

Attend as many CLE courses on this area as possible.

Absorb what you can from a mentor in this area.

_____

_____

_____

_____

_____

*An expert is someone who has succeeded in making decisions and*
*judgements simpler through knowing what to pay*
*attention to and what to ignore.*
EDWARD DE BONO

# Don't Expect from Others
# What You Could Not Deliver
# When You Were at Their Level of
# Professional Development

*None of us can stand other people having the same faults as ourselves.*
OSCAR WILDE

Most of us hold ourselves to high standards, just as we hold others to high standards as well. But a disconnect occurs when we forget the career timeline—you and your colleagues are engaged in a steady march toward more advanced professional development, but you didn't start out as fully developed. Often, we want to bring out the best in others and push them to raise the bar for themselves. The trick is not to forget that professional development is a progression. Where were you when you were at the same stage in your career as this person is now?

*Who is ever adequate? We all create situations each other can't live up to,*
*then break our hearts at them because they don't.*
ELIZABETH BOWEN

Practice improving your empathy for others.

Set realistic goals and expectations for others.

_____

_____

_____

*When the defects of others are perceived with so much clarity,*
*it is because one possesses them oneself.*
JULES RENARD

# Actively Supervise New Associates

*Good management consists in showing average people*
*how to do the work of superior people.*
JOHN D. ROCKEFELLER JR.

Stay engaged after delegating assignments. Consistent check-ins are a must for you to understand whether any unexpected challenges have arisen. Give teammates the freedom to do the work on their own and make them feel safe enough to seek help when needed. Avoid micromanaging. It screams "I don't trust you."

*How much supervision and control a firm should exert*
*over the work of an associate will depend, of course,*
*upon a continuing evaluation of his performance.*
*After he is hired, the partners will try to satisfy themselves*
*quickly about his legal intelligence*
*(the depth of his background in the law),*
*imagination (the unwillingness to accept any proposition*
*on the basis of its surface appeal),*
*organization (his accuracy, thoroughness,*
*and ability to get things done), and judgment.*
THEODORE VOORHEES

In addition to formal update meetings, informally check in with teammates to see how things are going.

Don't overreact when things start to go awry or fall behind. Provide constructive course-correction advice.

---

*Next to doing a good job yourself, the greatest joy is in having someone else*
*do a first-class job under your direction.*
WILLIAM FEATHER

# Don't Be Overly Critical

*Human error must be tolerated*
*because the price of perfection is prohibitive.*
EUGENE C. GERHART

If criticism is necessary, provide it in a constructive manner. Instead of tearing people down, find ways to build them up. Identifying ways a teammate can improve is an opportunity to build trust and accelerate their performance.

*Sandwich every bit of criticism*
*between two heavy layers of praise.*
MARY KAY ASH

Be aware of the words you use and the tone in which you deliver remarks when you're providing feedback.

Keep your tone constructive and upbeat to avoid blaming and browbeating.

_____

_____

_____

_____

_____

_____

_____

_____

*It is much easier to be critical than to be correct.*
BENJAMIN DISRAELI

# Don't Delegate Only Those Tasks You Hate to Do

*Delegating work works, provided the one delegating works, too.*
ROBERT HALF

Send the right message to your team by walking the talk and taking on some of the more unpleasant tasks in an engagement. Teammates rally around leaders who get in the trenches with them from time to time. Your actions speak volumes about your commitment to the overall success of the engagement.

*Delegation is an issue of respect and how much we respect those that are under us on our team.*
HANS FINZEL

After you have delegated the tasks for the engagement on paper, review the balance of the workload and difficulty of the tasks you have assigned.

Put yourself in your teammates' shoes and review what your role will look like for each task.

*Nothing is impossible for the man who doesn't have to do it himself.*
A. H. WEILER

# Share Insights with Newer Associates

*True leadership must be for the benefit of the followers,*
*not the enrichment of the leaders.*
ROBERT TOWNSEND

The best way to accelerate the performance of your team is to accelerate the careers of your teammates. Teach them insights today that you learned 5, 10 or 20 years into your career. They will appreciate it tremendously and you'll enjoy watching them grow as you reap the benefits of that growth.

*Law students can learn more from knowing*
*how to ask good questions than from studying appellate briefs.*
*To be able to make split-second decisions,*
*they have to feel law in their bones.*
ANTHONY G. AMSTERDAM

Share experience and insight in the moment when opportunities to do so arise.

_____

_____

_____

_____

_____

_____

_____

*Put knowledge where people trip over it.*
CARLA O'DELL

# Develop Your Supervisory Skills through Professional Development

*Outstanding leaders go out of their way to boost
the self-esteem of their personnel. If people believe in themselves,
it's amazing what they can accomplish.*
SAM WALTON

Be the leader you have followed or wish to follow. Learn the techniques and approaches that bring out the best in others.

*A good boss makes his men realize that have more ability than
they think they have so that they consistently
do better work than they thought they could.*
CHARLES ERWIN WILSON

Research and attend local professional development and leadership courses.

Imitate or mimic the techniques and approaches of the leaders you admire most.

_____

_____

_____

_____

_____

_____

*His motto, often followed but seldom expressed, was:
"Organize, delegate, supervise."*
ARTHUR T. VANDERBILT

## LEADING THE PACK

- Strive to Become an Expert in a Field
- Don't Expect from Others What You Could Not Deliver When You Were at Their Level of Professional Development
- Actively Supervise New Associates
- Don't Be Overly Critical
- Don't Delegate Only Those Tasks You Hate to Do
- Share Insights with Newer Associates
- Develop Your Supervisory Skills through Professional Development

# MARKETING SKILLS

For most attorneys, marketing is the most challenging area in the practice of law because it requires business skills that few attorneys possess, studied or find intuitive. The competition to secure engagements from new clients or existing ones is more intense than ever. As a result, attorneys must master the art and science of capturing more engagements for the firm. Having the ability to convert transactional engagements into relationship clients is a skill that can allow exponential growth to occur.

## MARKETING SKILLS

- Know Thyself, Market Thyself
- Spread the Word
- Be Choosy
- Understand the Easiest Market (Is the One You Already Have)
- Be the Face of the Firm
- Money Talks

# Know Thyself, Market Thyself

Marketing legal services starts with you. What do you personally bring to the table for this potential client? What does your firm offer over the competition? What will your role be in the engagement? From there, you build out the narrative on how you will directly or indirectly lead the team assigned to the engagement. This presentation in conversation must be concise and devoid of legal jargon so that potential clients can easily understand.

# Begin Networking Your First Day
# on the Job and Don't Stop Until You Retire

*If the house is on fire, forget the china, silver, and wedding album—*
*grab the Rolodex (database of contacts).*
HARVEY MACKAY

In a world filled with noise, it's difficult to retain relevancy because everyone and everything is easily forgotten. You must consistently stay in front of referral sources to maintain their awareness of you. In addition, assist referral sources with their needs so they reciprocate.

*The secret formula for getting clients is to remember*
*that every client is a human being. ...*
*The more number of people you know the greater*
*your chances of having a big clientele.*
*You will not get clients merely by putting up your board and*
*announcing proudly that you are a law graduate.*
R. K. SOONAVALA

Identify the clients you want to serve and the types of services your firm can provide to them.

Identify which other service providers work with these clients.

Join networking organizations where these service providers are members.

---

*Networking is the Nº. 1 unwritten rule of success in business.*
SALLIE KRAWCHECK

# Develop Your Own Clients

*None will improve your lot / If you yourselves do not.*
BERTOLT BRECHT

Institutional clients are great, but they can create a false sense of security. Within such clients, changes can occur that you have no control over, and in a moment the client moves their business elsewhere. Most transactions are personal in nature. People buy from people. The best clients are the ones who are directly connected to you. Unless you fail to meet their expectations with respect to legal services, these clients will stick with you wherever you practice law.

*A business never stands still. It either grows or decays.*
BENJAMIN N. CARDOZO

Go find your own clients and take control of your destiny.

_____

_____

_____

_____

_____

_____

_____

_____

*The greatest thing in the world is to know how to be self-sufficient.*
MICHEL DE MONTAIGNE

# Always Carry Your Business Cards with You

*Try not to become a person of success,*
*but rather try to become a person of value.*
ALBERT EINSTEIN

A business card is the oldest and easiest tool to use to help people remember you. You never know when an opportunity will arise from a meeting. Always employ a physical leave-behind. It helps you stay memorable and holds the promise of a future meeting.

*The business card is the most powerful single business tool—*
*dollar for dollar—you can invest in.*
IVAN MISNER

Keep a stash of business cards in your suit coat, purse, wallet, briefcase, car and home. You never know when you'll need to have your business cards handy.

---

*A good business card is one that leaves an impression,*
*and a bad one is one that gets lost.*
KAREN LELAND

# Establish and Maintain Relationships with Professionals Outside the Practice of Law

*Networking is marketing.*
*Marketing yourself, your uniqueness, marketing what you stand for.*
CHRISTINE COMAFORD-LYNCH

It's imperative that you journey outside the cocoon of legal services. Establish strong relationships with the other service providers for the clients you want to serve. Always remember that the purpose of networking is to help others advance their needs. The power of networking is in the reciprocation of your efforts.

*Too many individuals network to accomplish an immediate goal.*
*That's not networking. That's selling.*
UNKNOWN

Identify and join networking groups that include bankers, accountants, insurance agents and other service providers.

After briefly introducing yourself, ask, "How can I help you?" and "Who can I introduce you to?"

_____

_____

_____

_____

*The successful networkers I know, the ones receiving tons of referrals*
*and feeling truly happy about themselves, continually put the other person's*
*needs ahead of their own.*
BOB BURG

# Become a Member of Several Bar Organizations

*When you join a professional organization price is what you pay for membership. Value is what you get by becoming a participant.*
WENDELL M. PICHON

There is no better resource to stay current on CLE courses and trends in the practice of law than a bar organization. Get involved and interact with attorneys outside your firm. This will give you a better perspective.

*Your need for the Reports of the American Bar Association,*
*the American Bar Association Journal and your state and*
*local bar journals is obvious.*
*Without them you cannot know what is going on*
*in the administration of justice and in the legal profession.*
REGINALD HEBER SMITH

At a minimum, you should immediately join the local and state bar associations.

Joining a national bar association may make more sense later in your career.

_____

_____

_____

_____

*I believe we can accelerate our acumen, performance and success by*
*leveraging our associations and spending time with people better than us.*
ROBIN S. SHARMA

# Participate in Opportunities to Teach Your Craft

*To teach is to learn twice over.*
JOSEPH JOUBERT

Outside the practice of law itself, there's no better way to demonstrate your abilities and expertise than to get in front of an audience.

*The end and aim of a lawyer is duplex, first to know, and second to appear to know—the latter brings in clients and the former holds them.*
ROGER NORTH

Write articles, give speeches, teach a class and/or participate in seminar presentations.

_____

_____

_____

_____

_____

_____

_____

_____

_____

*It usually takes more than three weeks to prepare a good impromptu speech.*
MARK TWAIN

## KNOW THYSELF, MARKET THYSELF

- Begin Networking Your First Day on the Job and Don't Stop Until You Retire
- Develop Your Own Clients
- Always Carry Your Business Cards with You
- Establish and Maintain Relationships with Professionals Outside the Practice of Law
- Become a Member of Several Bar Organizations
- Participate in Opportunities to Teach Your Craft

# Spread the Word

Not only do you have to create awareness regarding your skills as an attorney and the value that you bring to the table for clients, but you must also do the same for the firm. Potential clients and referral sources need to know both your firm's and your perspective and experience after having solved nearly every problem imaginable with respect to a particular matter or issue. This requires persistence and an understanding of your role as one of the firm's ambassadors. Use the following tips and skills to spread the word about your firm and take your first steps as its most valuable ambassador.

# Know the Difference between
# Marketing and Selling

*The difference between Sales and Marketing is that Marketing owns
the message and Sales owns the relationship.*
JOHN JANTSCH

Marketing is strategic; selling is tactical. Marketing is building a brand for yourself and your firm. These brands set you and your firm apart from the commodity services that flood the market. Selling is the execution of the marketing strategy. The best and most loyal clients purchase based on brand.

*Fifty percent of Japanese companies do not have a marketing department,
and ninety percent have no special section for marketing research.
The reason is that everyone is considered to be a marketing specialist.*
HIROYUKI TAKEUCHI

Prepare a pitch deck for yourself and for your firm. Start with your "why" and build out "how" and "what" set you and your firm apart from the competition.

---

*A well-informed employee is the best salesperson a company can have.*
EDWIN J. THOMAS

# Put in Constant Effort to Market Effectively

*The fox that waited for the chickens to fall off their perch died of hunger.*
GREEK PROVERB

At times, marketing is as easy as pie. Other times, it is a grind. Regardless of the effort required, consistency is key. You can't let up on marketing yourself and your firm because you're in a marathon. If you let lag your efforts to bring perspective and value to the market, you will be forgotten.

*You will not get clients if you stay home six nights a week.*
HAROLD P. SELIGSON

Develop an annual networking strategy that you update quarterly when new opportunities arise to connect with potential clients and referral sources.

_____

_____

_____

_____

_____

_____

_____

_____

*Even if you are on the right track, you'll get run over if you just sit there.*
WILL ROGERS

# Continually Adapt to the Times

*Anything that won't sell, I don't want to invent.*
*A sale is proof of utility and utility is success.*
THOMAS A. EDISON

A law firm is driven by the market. You must pay attention to what the market is doing so you can service those new activities. We live and operate in a world that is constantly evolving and changing. You must adapt your practice to the times. If you don't, your practice will go the way of the dinosaurs.

*Men have not made inventions in business ...*
*men have not made economies in business to any great extent*
*because they wanted to.*
*They have made them because they had to,*
*and the proposition that "necessity is the mother of invention" is just as true*
*today in the time of the trust, in the era of the trust,*
*as it was hundreds of years before.*
ALPHEUS THOMAS MASON

Read broad-based blogs and periodicals such *The Kiplinger Letter* to stay abreast of industry trends.

Read local business journals (e.g., *Crain's*) and national publications (e.g., *Fortune*).

_____

_____

_____

_____

*No great marketing decisions have ever been made on quantitative data.*
JOHN SCULLEY

# Know What Sets Your Firm Apart from Other Law Firms

*Kodak sells film, but they don't advertise film,*
*they advertise memories.*
THEODORE LEVITT

If you can't articulate what sets your law firm apart from others, don't expect a potential client to figure it out on their own. Don't emphasize what you do. Emphasize the outcomes achieved and the strength and longevity of your client relationships. Demonstrate that your firm possesses the same values as the potential client.

*What sets you apart can sometimes feel like a burden and it's not.*
*And a lot of the time, it's what makes you great.*
EMMA STONE

The factor that sets you apart from the rest must be a part of your pitch deck.

Do your homework on the competition and know everything possible about your firm.

_____

_____

_____

_____

_____

_____

*In our factory, we make lipstick. In our advertising, we sell hope.*
CHARLES REVSON

# Don't Market Solely on Price: Boast of Your Firm's Expertise and Others' Recognition of It

*Cutting prices is usually insanity if the competition can go as low as you can.*
MICHAEL E. PORTER

If the conversation turns to who can do it for less, you're in a race to the bottom. You'll end up devaluing your firm's reputation and turning the firm and yourself into a commodity. You don't want these types of clients. They will never stop nickel-and-diming you.

*There is hardly anything in the world that some man cannot make a little worse and sell a little cheaper, and the people who consider price only are this man's lawful prey.*
JOHN RUSKIN

Although you must always disclose your fees, never allow this topic to be the center point of the conversation.

_____

_____

_____

_____

_____

*Anybody can cut prices, but it takes brains to make a better article.*
PHILIP D. ARMOUR

# Increase Your Firm's Visibility
# in the Community

*A desk is a dangerous place from which to watch the world.*
JOHN LE CARRÉ

Potential clients and referral sources aren't going to come running to you. By getting yourself out in the community and into networking events, you will slowly create curiosity and awareness. Networking is a process that must be engaged in consistently and expanded each year. The goal is to reach additional people while reinforcing the message with those who have already met you.

*We do not learn to know men through their coming to us.*
*To find out what sort of persons they are, we must go to them.*
JOHANN WOLFGANG VON GOETHE

Map out a plan each year to attend, participate in and contribute to community events.

Couple these efforts with your annual networking plan.

_____

_____

_____

_____

_____

_____

*The meek shall inherit the world, but they'll never increase market share.*
WILLIAM G. MCGOWAN

# Send Thank-You Cards to Clients and Referral Sources Promptly

*Courtesies of a small and trivial character are the ones which strike deepest in the grateful and appreciating heart.*
HENRY CLAY

The handwritten card or note has become a lost art. For that reason, the impact of sending one is better than ever. It takes only a minute to write and mail a personal message, and it will not get lost in a sea of junk emails. The recipient will appreciate it.

*Gratitude is the most exquisite form of courtesy.*
JACQUES MARITAIN

Acquire high-end thank-you cards and matching envelopes with the firm's logo on the front and blank on the inside.

Include your business card when you mail the thank-you to a referral or a client.

*To succeed in the world, you must also be well-mannered.*
VOLTAIRE

# Develop a Creative Approach to Marketing

*Follow the crowd and you will never be followed by a crowd.*
ANONYMOUS

Presenting your firm in the same manner as the competition screams "we're a commodity!" Once a potential client senses that you are a commodity, the conversation will immediately go to who can do the work for the lowest fee. That's not where you want to be.

*Instead of resisting the trend toward popular marketing and*
*professional services ... [we] should encourage and shape it.*
*The public needs the professional equivalent of Chevrolets*
*as well as Cadillacs.*
DOUG HARLAN

Present your firm in a manner that highlights expertise, experience and value-add.

Share stories, without breaching confidentiality, to enable a client to relate.

Discuss the longevity and depth of relationship of similar clients.

_____

_____

_____

_____

_____

_____

*A person who walks in another's tracks leaves no footprints.*
ANONYMOUS

143

## SPREAD THE WORD

- Know the Difference between Marketing and Selling
- Put in Constant Effort to Market Effectively
- Continually Adapt to the Times
- Know What Sets Your Firm Apart from Other Law Firms
- Don't Market Solely on Price: Boast of Your Firm's Expertise and Others' Recognition of It
- Increase Your Firm's Visibility in the Community
- Send Thank-You Cards to Clients and Referral Sources Promptly
- Develop a Creative Approach to Marketing

# Be Choosy

New clients are the lifeblood of any practice. Acquiring new clients is the best way to fuel growth and fight off decline simultaneously. You need to keep a constant eye out for opportunities by positioning yourself and your firm in the right circles. Although you should actively pursue opportunities, don't be too aggressive in your approach to land a potential client. Also, be sure to exercise discretion in choosing clients. To ensure that new relationships start off on the right foot, both parties must disclose sufficient information so that expectations are reasonable and there are no unpleasant surprises between attorney and client.

# Choose Clients Carefully

*He that lies down with dogs shall rise up with fleas.*
LATIN PROVERB

Just as you are a reflection of them, clients are a reflection of you and your firm. They can raise you up or bring you down in stature and thinking.

*Be aware of the company you keep.*
*You'd be surprised how easily they rub off on you.*
*You don't want to attract the wrong influence.*
AMAKA IMANI NKOSAZANA

Do your homework regarding potential clients.

Google them and gather any information you can find.

Go into an engagement with eyes wide open.

---

*Tell me with whom you associate, and I will tell you who you are.*
JOHANN WOLFGANG VON GOETHE

# Focus Your Efforts on Serving Those Enterprises That Are on the Cutting Edge of Their Industry

*Lots of people know a good thing the minute the other fellow sees it first.*
JOB E. HEDGES

Finding cutting-edge clients is where networking with the right referral sources is critical. Creating awareness of your firm directly with founders in specific entrepreneurial circles is equally important. To get your foot in the door with start-ups, you will likely have to perform some pro bono work or provide services at a reduced fee until the enterprise is on solid ground. Showing up second or after the risk of failure is low is too late.

*If you want to hit a bird on the wing,*
*you must have all your will in a focus,*
*you must not be thinking about yourself,*
*and, equally, you must not be thinking about your neighbor;*
*you must be living in your eye on that bird.*
*Every achievement is a bird on the wing.*
OLIVER WENDELL HOLMES JR.

Consistently network within entrepreneurial organizations and with venture capital firms.

*All strategy depends on competition.*
BRUCE D. HENDERSON

# Make the Client Aware of
# the Cost of Your Firm's Legal Services
# Before You Begin Representation

*Personally, I like to know what the bill is going to be before I order a luxury.*
OLIVER WENDELL HOLMES JR.

A well-drafted engagement letter that sets expectations for a client is critical. When it comes to fees, it's imperative that the client is in agreement on the costs incurred. Make sure each client receives a detailed billing that lists the time used, the rate applied and a description of the services provided. Do everything you can to avoid surprising clients with the fees.

*I see how attorneys are, and nobody is really on your side.*
*It's about money. The attorney is not chasing after your money,*
*he's chasing after his fee.*
MANNIE FRESH

At the start of the engagement, everything must be in writing, countersigned and understood.

_____

_____

_____

_____

_____

*The price is what you pay. Value is what you get.*
WARREN BUFFET

# Don't Be Afraid to Offer Your Services
# When the Opportunity to Do So Arises

*A bashful beggar has an empty purse.*
HUNGARIAN PROVERB

Ask for the order. Point out when value can be added during an engagement. Don't expect the client to figure it out on their own.

*If you want to make money, you have to help someone else make money.*
RUSSELL SIMMONS

Understand how your client makes money.

Connect the dots on how your services can help your client be more profitable.

_____

_____

_____

_____

_____

_____

_____

_____

_____

_____

*Many things are lost for want of asking.*
ENGLISH PROVERB

# Know When to Use the "Soft Sell"

Pushing too hard gives the impression that there is more in it for you than for your client.

Use questions more than statements in these situations.

Make it all about the client.

# Know How to Close the Sale and Bring a New Client into the Fold

*In science the credit goes to the man who convinces the world,*
*not to the man to whom the idea first occurs.*
SIR WILLIAM OSLER

In the end, your ability to persuade will pull the potential client across the line. How well you emotionally connect with the prospect will likely dictate the likelihood and speed of securing them as a new client.

*If you stop adding new clients, you start bleeding to death.*
DAVID OGILVY

Remember, more times than not, people make decisions based on emotions and then rationalize their choices with financial analysis.

_____

_____

_____

_____

_____

_____

*To earn the respect (and eventually love) of your customers,*
*you first have to respect those customers.*
*That is why Golden Rule behavior is embraced by most winning companies.*
COLLEEN BARRETT

## BE CHOOSY

- Choose Clients Carefully
- Focus Your Efforts on Serving Those Enterprises That Are on the Cutting Edge of Their Industry
- Make the Client Aware of the Cost of Your Firm's Legal Services Before You Begin Representation
- Don't Be Afraid to Offer Your Services When the Opportunity to Do So Arises
- Know When to Use the "Soft Sell"
- Know How to Close the Sale and Bring a New Client into the Fold

# Understand the Easiest Market (Is the One You Already Have)

Post-retention, if you do not develop and implement certain skills, a new client will begin to perceive that their business is being taken for granted or that the relationship is merely transactional. This may lead the client to turn to other firms for future legal counsel. The opportunity cost to the law firm includes not only the loss of an existing client but also that of an excellent referral source.

More times than not, such a turn of events can be avoided. Never forget the timeless axiom that it is five to seven times more costly to generate business from a new client than it is to do business with an existing one. Add five to seven times the value to your firm by using the following skills to retain the clients you already have.

# Keep Existing Clients Happy

*The easiest and most powerful way to increase customer loyalty is really
very simple. Make your customers happy.*
KEVIN STIRTZ

Numerous studies over many years have consistently concluded
that it costs five to seven times more to find a new client than
it does to retain an existing one. Always know where you stand
with your clients and course-correct whenever required to keep
them happy.

*Four little words sum up what has lifted
most successful individuals above the crowd: a little bit more.
They did all that was expected of them and a little bit more.*
A. LOU VICKERY

Check in with clients from time to time. Ask for feedback, rec-
ommendations and whether you are meeting their expectations.

Stay engaged and understand how they see your performance.

---

---

---

---

---

---

*Why is it that there is never enough time to do a job right,
but always time enough to do it over?*
ANONYMOUS

# Treat Every Client Like
# They Are Your Firm's Most Important
# Client—They Are

*Small opportunities are often the beginning of great enterprises.*
DEMOSTHENES

Clients need to feel appreciated. The thought that they are being taken for granted or treated like a second-tier client cannot happen. It's up to you to demonstrate how much you and the firm appreciate their business. Take the initiative to do so often.

*Courteous treatment will make a customer a walking advertisement.*
JAMES CASH PENNY

Express your appreciation for your clients' business regularly.

Invite clients to social events.

Show sincere interest in your clients' affairs.

_____

_____

_____

_____

_____

_____

_____

*Nobody cares how much you know, until they know how much you care.*
THEODORE ROOSEVELT

# Keep Your Clients Informed of Recent Changes in the Law That May Affect Their Business

*Get closer than ever to your customers. So [you can]*
*... tell them what they need ... before they realize it.*
STEVE JOBS

Keeping clients apprised of legal changes that affect them is a great approach that adds value for your clients. If you understand their business and you keep on top of new developments that can affect their business, you can look out for them. Clients appreciate this.

*A moment's insight is sometimes worth a life's experience.*
OLIVER WENDELL HOLMES SR.

Add your clients to update notices and monthly newsletters published by the firm.

Keep an eye out for changes in the law that will affect your clients. Share the information with them and discuss it.

_____

_____

_____

_____

_____

*Be dramatically willing to focus on the customer at all costs,*
*even at the cost of obsoleting your own stuff.*
SCOTT D. COOK

# Add Value to Your Client's Business through Your Services and Business Relationships

If you're in the practice of law just for the money, you'll never make it. If you genuinely put the customer first, you'll end up providing extraordinary service and searching for ways to enrich their business. In turn, you'll be rewarded with an extraordinary relationship.

Make introductions.

Ask clients how you can help beyond the services you provide.

Continually think of how other services the firm offers will grow your client's business.

_____

_____

_____

_____

_____

# Assign Matters to Those Professionals Who Can Provide the Needed Services the Most Cost-Effectively

*People forget how fast you did a job—*
*but they remember how well you did it.*
HOWARD W. NEWTON

On-the-job training is a critical component of professional development. Clients, however, don't want to pay in full for an attorney's education. Assign your best teammates to each engagement and make sure that the process is managed efficiently.

*While a law firm is not a business in the ordinary commercial sense,*
*it is nonetheless a business, and it must be managed accordingly.*
*The foundation of every successful law practice is*
*an efficient business system.*
JAMES E. BRILL

Keep a close eye on the time spent on the tasks for an engagement.

Write off inefficiencies (time) before invoicing the client.

_____

_____

_____

_____

_____

*Lawyers do not unfairly charge their clients.*
*Rather they simply do not dispense legal services efficiently.*
JAMES D. FELLERS

# Practice Development and
# Marketing Are Not Mutually Exclusive

*Networking is marketing.*
*Marketing yourself, marketing your uniqueness,*
*marketing what you stand for.*
CHRISTINE COMAFORD-LYNCH

The better you get, the easier it is to market your services (build your brand). Continuous learning and professional improvement make you more attractive to potential clients. Most importantly, create awareness of your development with your clients.

*I tell you that as long as I can conceive something better*
*than myself, I cannot be easy unless I am striving to bring it*
*into existence or clearing the way for it.*
GEORGE BERNARD SHAW

Keep your LinkedIn and firm profiles updated to reflect recent accomplishments.

Share updates with clients in casual conversation.

*In order to compose, all you need is to remember a tune that*
*nobody else has thought of.*
ROBERT SCHUMANN

# Don't Forget Who Pays the Bills

*When a customer enters my store, forget me. He is king.*
JOHN WANAMAKER

The client is not always literally right. A better description of the relationship is "the client is always in control." You need to lead the engagement and, yes, you're in charge of the engagement. If push comes to shove, however, the client can pull the plug at any time.

*The customer is always right.*
H. GORDON SELFRIDGE

Never forget this dynamic of who is in control of what and understand your place.

Build goodwill with your clients.

---

*Goodwill is the one and only asset that*
*competition cannot undersell or destroy.*
MARSHALL FIELD

## UNDERSTAND THE EASIEST MARKET (IS THE ONE YOU ALREADY HAVE)

- Keep Existing Clients Happy
- Treat Every Client Like They Are Your Firm's Most Important Client—They Are
- Keep Your Clients Informed of Recent Changes in the Law That May Affect Their Business
- Add Value to Your Client's Business through Your Services and Business Relationships
- Assign Matters to Those Professionals Who Can Provide the Needed Services the Most Cost-Effectively
- Practice Development and Marketing Are Not Mutually Exclusive
- Don't Forget Who Pays the Bills

# Be the Face of the Firm

Creating favorable perceptions of your firm among clients is the area where your people skills and emotional quotient (EQ) are so important. Your ability to read the room, effectively communicate and properly interact with clients enables you to create a tremendous bond with your clients. Mastering the following skills will raise your stature in the eyes of your clients. You will no longer be viewed as just an individual attorney.

# Relish Client Contact

*Ask your customers to be part of the solution,*
*and don't view them as part of the problem.*
ALAN WEISS

Every time you speak or write to a client, it's an opportunity for you and your team to shine. Include your client in the process. This is how you build rapport. Being with clients is your moment in the spotlight onstage.

*Do what you do so well that they will want to see it again and*
*bring their friends.*
WALT DISNEY

Stay in communication with your clients.

Keep them engaged and informed.

Seek feedback throughout the engagement and listen carefully.

---
---
---
---
---
---
---
---

*The more you engage with customers, the clearer things become and the*
*easier it is to determine what you should be doing.*
JOHN RUSSELL

# Personally Greet Clients in the Reception Area—Don't Have Your Secretary Bring Them to You

*Respect is a two-way street.*
*If you want to get it, you've got to give it.*
R. G. RISCH

Actions speak louder than words. You serve the client. Act like it. Demonstrate your respect for the client and appreciation of the engagement through your actions. It's their circus and you should be grateful for the opportunity to perform in it.

*Respecting someone indicates the quality of your personality.*
MOHAMMAD SAKHI

Demonstrate your respect for your client every chance you get.

Be self-aware of your statements and actions that affect clients.

_____

_____

_____

_____

_____

_____

*Respect for ourselves guides our morals,*
*respect for others guides our manners.*
LAURENCE STERNS

# Return All Communications
# within Two Hours

We're all busy. I get it. But clients don't like to be left waiting indefinitely for a response. Make it a priority to get back to your clients quickly when they've contacted you. Try not to ever keep clients hanging on wondering when they'll hear back from you.

*Unless there is an emergency call, why not bunch our phone calls?*
*That will keep me from popping up every time the phone rings.*
*Tell them I'll call back later.*
PETER J. STEINCROHN

If you're tied up in deposition, in a closing or in court , state that in your voicemail message and out-of-office reply.

Make replies a priority.

---

# Learn How to Put Clients at Ease.
# A Little Hand-Holding Goes a Long Way

*Happiness has many roots, but none more important than security.*
E. R. STETTINIUS JR.

When things get uneasy, your "bedside manner" needs to be employed. Clients need to be reassured, at times, or provided an update on what the financial exposure really looks like. Remember that all engagements have some level of discomfort for your client.

*Ease your customer's pain.*
HAZEL EDWARDS

Demonstrate some empathy.

Ask the client how they feel.

Share the information that's needed to alleviate some of their anxiety.

_____

_____

_____

_____

_____

_____

_____

*A man of calm is like a shady tree. People who need shelter come to it.*
TOBA BETA

# Don't Become Impatient in Front of Clients

*Calmness is always Godlike.*
RALPH WALDO EMERSON

Clients are paying for your time. Give it to them, as much as is required. If they are having a hard time understanding an issue or the next steps, perhaps the problem is your delivery.

*Impatience can cause wise people to do foolish things.*
JANETTE OKE

Be mindful of the things that make you impatient.

Practice gratitude.

Don't be quick to react.

---

*The twin killers of success are impatience and greed.*
JIM ROHN

# When Socializing with Clients, Keep Talk About Business and Law to a Minimum

*There are worse things in life than death.*
*Have you ever spent an evening with an insurance salesman?*
WOODY ALLEN

Social events are an opportunity to show a different side of yourself to a client. Have some fun. Clients may wonder what you're like outside the office. Social settings provide you with a chance to connect on a different level with your client and find new areas of commonality.

*Put human interest into your talk.*
*It is a universal truism that people are interested*
*in people rather than things.*
*To inject human interest,*
*talk about people with whom your listeners can identify themselves.*
HARRY SIMMONS

Develop hobbies and interests outside of work.

Become familiar with and knowledgeable about things that you have a passion for and that others find interesting as well.

---

---

---

*Yes, I guess you could say I am a loner, but I feel more lonely in a crowded*
*room with boring people than I feel on my own.*
HENRY ROLLINS

# Clients Aren't Impressed with Legal Jargon, So Speak English

*Incomprehensible jargon is the hallmark of a profession.*
KINGMAN BREWSTER JR.

When speaking to your colleagues, use all the jargon you want. When speaking to clients, don't use any jargon. You're not impressing anyone and you will lose your audience quickly. If you can't explain something simply, it means you don't understand it well.

*Our business is infested with idiots*
*who try to impress by using pretentious jargon.*
DAVID OGILVY

Eradicate jargon from all client communication.

Use the everyday English equivalent in place of jargon.

*One of the main functions of jargon is to exaggerate expertise.*
MOKOKOMA MOKHONOANA

# Thoroughly Explain the Possible Consequences of Matters to Clients

*Neither Law nor Human Nature is an exact science.*
GEORGE W. KEETON

Clients don't like surprises. Nearly all are risk averse on some level. As a result, clients need to know what's at stake at all times.

*Take calculated risks. That is quite different from being rash.*
GEORGE S. PATTON

Thoroughly evaluate all the possibilities based on probabilities and share the information with your client.

_____

_____

_____

_____

_____

_____

_____

_____

_____

_____

_____

*Life is very singularly made to surprise us*
*(where is does not utterly appall us).*
RAINER MARIA RILKE

# Learn to Instill Confidence in Your Clients without Creating a Sense of False Hope

*Optimism is the faith that leads to achievement.*
*Nothing can be done without hope and confidence.*
HELEN KELLER

Remember that confidence is not a set of rules—it's a state of mind. Clients don't initially feel confident about the outcome of a new or potentially difficult situation. By building your client's belief in your ability, skills and experience, you will instill confidence in your clients.

*Sooner or later, those who win are those who think they can.*
PAUL TOURNIER

Let clients know that "you've been here before" and that you have the skills and capabilities to reach a successful outcome. It will go a long way to building their confidence.

Find the sources of your client's unease so you can address them.

_____

_____

_____

_____

_____

_____

*False hope is a terrible thing.*
*If it is the only thing keeping you alive, you'll be dead by dawn.*
CHARLIE RAE

# Don't Breach a Client's Confidence

*O fie, miss, you must not kiss and tell.*
WILLIAM CONGREVE

The foundation of client rapport is trust. You must never do or say something that gives the impression that you're untrustworthy. You could lose a client in an instant in such a circumstance. This is more than just an ethical issue. If you always conduct yourself in a rock-solid manner, the bond between you and your client will only continue to strengthen.

*I usually get my stuff from people who promised*
*somebody else that they would keep a secret.*
WALTER WINCHELL

Keep your mouth shut. Don't talk in your sleep. End of conversation.

_____

_____

_____

_____

_____

_____

_____

*We should never forget that most people know*
*something that almost everybody else doesn't know and*
*they are dying to pass it along.*
WILLIAM SAFIRE

# Go the Extra Mile for Your Clients

You can't just "show up" or "phone it in" if you want to produce extraordinary outcomes or be deemed one of the best in your field. More times than not, discipline and perseverance over intellect make the difference in the outcome. Simply put, hard work is a reflection of your commitment.

Effectively plan every engagement. Push hard to meet each benchmark.

Celebrate small successes and wins.

Log your accomplishments and the setbacks you have overcome.

_____

_____

_____

_____

_____

_____

# Show Enthusiasm for Your Clients' Successes

*You are not the hero. Your customer makes their own success.*
BRIAN GLADSTEIN

You must adopt the mindset that you are on your clients' team outside the legal services you are providing. Take the focus off of you. It's about them. Celebrate their successes!

*As a leader, it is important to not just see your own success*
*but focus on the success of others.*
SUNDAR PICHAI

Pay attention to your clients' business.

Be one of the first to congratulate a client on their successes.

_____

_____

_____

_____

_____

_____

_____

_____

_____

_____

_____

*There are no uninteresting things, there are only uninterested people.*
GILBERT K. CHESTERTON

# Always Produce Results for Your Clients

Clients retain attorneys to achieve outcomes. Full stop.

List primary and secondary goals for an engagement.

Measure performance against these desired outcomes throughout the engagement.

## BE THE FACE OF THE FIRM

- Relish Client Contact
- Personally Greet Clients in the Reception Area—Don't Have Your Secretary Bring Them to You
- Return All Communications within Two Hours
- Learn How to Put Clients at Ease. A Little Hand-Holding Goes a Long Way
- Don't Become Impatient in Front of Clients
- When Socializing with Clients, Keep Talk About Business and Law to a Minimum
- Clients Aren't Impressed by Legal Jargon, So Speak English
- Thoroughly Explain the Possible Consequences of Matters to Clients
- Learn to Instill Confidence in Your Clients without Creating a Sense of False Hope
- Don't Breach a Client's Confidence
- Go the Extra Mile for Your Clients
- Show Enthusiasm for Your Clients' Successes
- Always Produce Results for Your Clients

# Money Talks

Nobody wants to get ripped off. Clients want to receive their money's worth. In every engagement there is a level of trust that is transferred from the client to his or her attorney. Clients trust that you will conduct yourself ethically and represent their interests with integrity. When it comes to fees and expenses, an attorney should never be tempted to charge a radical or risky fee for short-term gain. Holding yourself to the highest standards in every aspect of the practice of law pays the greatest dividends.

# Don't Guarantee Results to Clients

There are no guarantees in the practice of law, only probabilities. No matter how strong the case or supporting fact pattern, Murphy's Law can always come back to bite you.

Present outcomes to your clients in terms of probabilities, such as *fair*, *good*, *strong*. It's best not to use numerical percentages. Too many unknowns could arise that prevent you from accurately prognosticating an outcome.

_____

_____

_____

_____

_____

_____

_____

_____

# If Possible, Purchase Your Clients' Products or Services

*I honestly don't think twice about a relationship with people*
*who don't reciprocate respect.*
PORSHA WILLIAMS

The Law of Reciprocity is simple. When someone does something for you, you'll feel obligated to do something in return for them. It's a simple way to demonstrate mutual support.

*I always use my clients' products.*
*This is not toadyism, but elementary good manners.*
*Almost everything I consume is manufactured by one of my clients.*
DAVID OGILVY

Look for opportunities to support your client's business.

_____

_____

_____

_____

_____

_____

_____

_____

*A little reciprocity goes a long way.*
MALCOM FORBES

# Never Create Unnecessary Work
## at the Client's Expense

*We work not only to produce but to give value to time.*
EUGÈNE DELACROIX

Put yourself in the shoes of your client. The engagement is a cost of doing business (e.g., litigation), a part of life (e.g., estate planning) or a means to acquire an asset (e.g., business sale). Going into the engagement, the client is expecting to achieve a desired outcome in the fastest and most efficient manner. They don't want to be bogged down with sidebar matters that aren't relevant to their goals.

*In a bureaucratic system, useless work drives out useful work.*
MILTON FRIEDMAN

Review each action and document in the engagement plan.

Critically evaluate whether each item is required to achieve the desired outcome.

Do the same before running down a rabbit hole midstream during the engagement.

*It just seems so useless to have to work so hard and nothing ever really seems to come from it.*
TOM PETTY

# When Traveling at the Client's Expense, Fly Coach and Eat at Moderately Priced Restaurants

*Business is other people's money.*
DELPHINE DE GIRARDIN

The expense account for an engagement is not a blank check the client writes. Frugality goes a long way with clients. Lack thereof has the opposite effect and will likely hurt your relationship.

*The first thing you've got to remember is that it's*
*your client's money that you're spending.*
RICHARD MORRIS HUNT

Prior to incurring expenses, confirm that (1) they are necessary and (2) the same outcome cannot be reasonably achieved for less money.

_____

_____

_____

_____

_____

_____

_____

*Spending money is much more difficult than making money.*
JACK MA

# Don't Gouge Your Clients.
# Anticipate and Satisfy All of Your Clients'
# Needs Cost-Effectively

Next to incompetence, the perception of being ripped off will bring a client relationship to a screeching halt. The market offers many choices to clients. They won't tolerate overbilling.

Have a historical benchmark for what the expected fees will be and communicate this information to the client at the start of the engagement.

If unexpected events occur that increase your fees, make the client aware of them immediately.

# Always Confirm That the Amount Your Client Could Be Billed Is Not Disproportionate to the Value Your Firm Can Provide

*Getting your money's worth is not enough.*
*Get your heart and mind's worth.*
STEVEN DIETZ

At times, your firm will not be the right one for an engagement owing to the economics. This is when you need to speak up and recommend another firm, typically a sole practitioner, who can perform the work at a much lower fee. Clients will appreciate the introduction under such circumstances.

*Earn with your mind, not your time.*
NAVAL RAVIKANT

Before taking on an engagement, compare your expected legal fees and expenses to the value your client will obtain.

_____

_____

_____

_____

_____

_____

_____

*A nickel ain't worth a dime anymore.*
YOGI BERRA

## MONEY TALKS

- ◆ Don't Guarantee Results to Clients
- ◆ If Possible, Purchase Your Clients' Products or Services
- ◆ Never Create Unnecessary Work at the Client's Expense
- ◆ When Traveling at the Client's Expense, Fly Coach and Eat at Moderately Priced Restaurants
- ◆ Don't Gouge Your Clients. Anticipate and Satisfy All of Your Client's Needs Cost-Effectively
- ◆ Always Confirm That the Amount Your Client Could Be Billed Is Not Disproportionate to the Value Your Firm Can Provide

# Conclusion

Thank you for purchasing this book and congratulations on taking the time to read it! Please be sure to properly reflect on the advice and complete the activities and assignments for each skill. I firmly belief that when you incorporate the skills listed in each chapter, you will advance your career at an exponentially accelerated rate.

Clearly, you are dedicated to becoming a well-rounded attorney who desires to add exceptional value to your firm. You are now on the path to becoming an irreplaceable ambassador for your firm. Stay the course!

Beyond the substantive law and matters of procedure, the practice of law is multifaceted. Much of the knowledge and skill that is required to be successful is not taught in law school, nor is it intuitive. What you'll discover is that regardless of whether it's a general skill, a legal skill or a marketing skill, it almost always boils down to people and understanding the dynamics of an engagement and being able to read the room. You must know how to respond to, inspire, influence, manage and motivate others to be a successful attorney. Overarching people skills take years to master and must be continually practiced.

As you look to the horizon, expect many rewarding events to transpire throughout your career. Not all will be prominent. But relish all of them regardless of their size or impact and have some fun! I wish you the best on your journey.

# About the Author

Jeff Baldassari practiced law from 1990 to 1995 with the national law firm of BakerHostetler LLP in its Cleveland office. His areas of concentration included creditors' rights, business law and real estate law. At the time of this book's original writing in 1993, BakerHostetler was the 23rd-largest law firm in the United States, with approximately 450 attorneys located in eight offices. In 2023, BakerHostetler remains an AmLaw 50 firm, with over a thousand attorneys in 17 offices.

For more than two decades, Jeff served as president and CEO of two manufacturing companies and as a director on six boards in the private sector and nonprofit sector. He has been a client of legal services across a multitude of practice areas. His unique career path has given him the opportunity to see and experience the practice of law as both a provider and a recipient.